MW01094125

# Auditing that Matters

## Norman Marks, CPA, CRMA

© Norman Marks, 2016, all rights reserved

# Table of Contents

## Introduction

I am a great believer in the value to an organization of an effective internal audit department. That should not surprise anybody, as I have been an internal audit practitioner for the majority of my working life.

I have a passion for internal auditing and spend a good amount of my time, now that I am retired, writing and speaking on the topic. This book is designed to build on my previous work (which includes my 2014 book, *World-Class Internal Audit: Tales from my Journey*, published articles, and several hundred blog posts) and explain my thinking on how internal audit can and should be of immense value to any organization.

Over the last years, significant progress has been made in the professional practice of internal auditing, especially when it comes to risk-based auditing. I especially like some of the new Core Principles for effective internal auditing that were adopted by the Institute of Internal Auditors in 2015[1]. They include the principles that internal audit:

- ❑ Communicates effectively
- ❑ Provides risk-based assurance
- ❑ Is insightful, proactive, and future-focused
- ❑ Promotes organizational improvement

At first sight, these seem to represent what internal audit departments across the globe are doing now, in 2016. I am not so sure.

Is internal auditing communicating, in an appropriately timely manner that supports decision-making by the board and management team, whether the risks that matter to the success of the organization are managed as desired?

---

[1] The Core Principles were included in the update of the International Professional Practices Framework (IPPF), as recommended by the IIA's Relook Task Force, of which I was privileged to be a member.

Is internal auditing really thinking about the road ahead and the risks around the corner, or is it focused mainly on past activity and current capability?

Is it effective, as effective as it can and should be, in helping the organization bring its systems, processes, organizational structure, and people to the desired level of performance?

In some departments, the answer may be "yes". But, I believe the number of such world-class departments is small.

As I wrote in my 2014 book, my thinking and practice of effective internal auditing developed over a number of years. I hope in the pages that follow to explain where I am now and provide some ideas and practical suggestions that will lead more departments to perform at world-class levels.

## Chapter 1: What is auditing that matters?

How often does the new CEO of an organization make it a priority to meet with the Chief Audit Executive (CAE) in his first week? Surely, an effective CAE can provide the new CEO with objective insight into the management team, organization, systems, and processes that the CEO has inherited.

It is more likely that the CEO will see the internal audit function as a "necessary evil", an expense that has to be incurred to satisfy regulations and such or to keep the audit committee members happy.

He may see the CAE as somebody who will tell him when there are problems, but usually not as a key partner in leading the organization to success.

When KPMG completed its 2015 *Global Audit Committee Survey*, they reported that "Fewer than half of the 1,800 respondents are satisfied that internal audit delivers the value to the company it should (45%), and that the internal audit plan properly focuses on the 'critical risks to the enterprise' (49%)".

It's not only that these audit committee members were less than satisfied that they were getting full value; about half of them said that internal audit was not addressing the risks that matter to the enterprise as a whole – the critical risks to its success. If internal audit had a contribution to make to the likelihood of the organization achieving its objectives, such as pointing out issues that might derail such achievement or opportunities to enhance results, surely the full board would want to know – and ensure appropriate action is taken by management.

PwC found similar results in its 2015 annual report on the State of the Profession. Their comment was that "expectations have risen, and all internal audit functions need to rise to this new floor: providing assurance on a broader range of critical risks and clearly communicating deeper insights."

New Zealand is seen by many as quite progressive in its governance and risk management practices. Yet, a member of multiple boards of companies based there and a former deputy CEO[2] said this:

> "Almost all of IA findings are mundane operational compliance issues"

When internal audit is seen as auditing areas that are not on the board agenda and are not critical to the success of the organization, their work may be 'important' but doesn't really matter.

When internal audit is seen as lacking the ability to address some of the more critical business risks, such as cyber security or organizational culture, the board and top management are not going to look to them for assurance in those areas.

In 2015, I spoke at a number of events organized by the National Association of Corporate Directors. The NACD brought together members of the boards of US organizations, large and small, to discuss cyber security risks. When one director shared her view that internal audit was not competent to address the issue, all the others present agreed immediately.

That is a sad and disturbing reality. It may only be perception, but that is enough.

For internal audit to 'matter', it needs to:

1. Focus on the risks that matter to the board and top management – risks to the successful delivery of value to stakeholders, the achievement of objectives set by the board.

2. Provide assurance on those risks that is readily consumable, relevant, actionable, and timely – helping board members and executives make informed decisions that lead the organization to success; where action is necessary, it can be taken promptly and effectively.

---

[2] Drew Stein has been a member of multiple boards, a senior executive, and is now CEO of a consulting company in New Zealand.

3. The form of internal audit assurance should be a formal opinion[3] by the CAE on whether the systems of internal control and risk management provide reasonable assurance that the more significant risks are managed at desired levels.

4. In addition to formal assurance, internal audit needs to provide its objective insight on any area critical to the achievement of success. For example, internal audit cannot be fearful of sharing its opinion on the performance of key personnel, the structure of the organization, and so on.

5. Communicate *what* its stakeholders need to know, *when* they need to know, and *in a form* that is easily consumed, relevant, and actionable.

6. Work effectively with management to assist them upgrade their processes, systems, organizational structure, controls, and people as needed.

These six points are consistent with the four IIA's Principles quoted in the Introduction. The IIA has additional Core Principles that enable internal audit to perform at this level. They state that an effective internal audit department:

❑ Demonstrates integrity

❑ Demonstrates competence and due professional care

❑ Is objective and free from undue influence (independent)

❑ Aligns with the strategies, objectives, and risks of the organization

❑ Is appropriately positioned and adequately resourced

❑ Demonstrates quality and continuous improvement

---

[3] See The Overall Opinion in Chapter 9 for more details

All of these are fundamental to an effective internal audit function. They provide a foundation for internal audit performance[4].

But for internal audit to matter to the board and top executives, it needs to <u>deliver</u> on the six points above.

What does a world-class internal audit function, one that matters, look like? Let me illustrate by sharing what my key stakeholders said about internal audit when I was CAE at Tosco Corporation.

- The chairman of the audit committee of the board said that internal audit "helped him sleep through the night". Our work provided him and the rest of the audit committee with the assurance they needed that the more significant risks were being adequately addressed by management – not only those risks facing the organization today, but those in their path forward.

   Internal audit helped the audit committee fulfil their oversight responsibilities.

- The CFO told the audit committee that if they wanted to know what was really happening they should "ask internal audit". During the closing meeting for our review of a major systems implementation, the IT department and the primary users were at each other's throats, blaming each other for the problems they were facing. The CFO calmly looked to the internal audit lead for an objective perspective – which all present respected.

   We helped the CFO in his leadership role.

- Tosco had two divisions: the Marketing Company ran the roughly 6,000 convenience stores (primarily under the company-owned Circle K brand) and gas stations (most of which were branded as Union 76, a brand owned by Tosco). The President of Tosco Marketing Company told a visiting politician that "internal audit

---

[4] Internal audit may not be given the opportunity to succeed by a board and CEO that are weak. I have seen situations where they hire a CAE just to "check the box" and say that have an internal audit function. But the CAE has neither the resources nor the capability to succeed. This book assumes that exemplary performance will be recognized.

helped the company stay efficient" – a critical task given the very low margins it was able to generate.

- The Refining Company ran nine oil refineries (making Tosco the third largest U.S. refiner, behind only ExxonMobil and BP), pipelines, and wholesale terminals. The President of the Refining Company told the Governor of the state of New Jersey that "internal audit gave Tosco a competitive advantage". Not only did we provide him the assurance he needed to run the business with confidence in its processes, systems, and personnel, but we also helped keep costs down by auditing major contractors.

Internal audit mattered to our stakeholders because we helped them be successful.

The first step on the path to this level of success is to know where and what to audit. What are the risks that our engagements should focus on? What are the risks that matter?

## Risk Based Internal Auditing

In 2003, the IIA UK published an excellent Position Paper on risk-based internal auditing (RBIA). As I will explain later, I now prefer to talk about *enterprise* risk-based internal auditing to indicate the focus on enterprise risks. However, the UK paper makes some excellent points that are worth referencing at this point.

The objective of RBIA is to provide independent assurance to the board that:

- The risk management processes which management has put in place within the organisation (covering all risk management processes at corporate, divisional, business unit, business process level, etc.) are operating as intended.

- These risk management processes are of sound design.

- The responses which management has made to risks which they wish to treat are both adequate and effective in reducing those risks to a level acceptable to the board.

11

- And a sound framework of controls is in place to sufficiently mitigate those risks which management wishes to treat.

The paper continues with:

> RBIA starts with the business objectives and then focuses on those risks that have been identified by management that may hinder their achievement.

There is more in the Paper that merits consideration, and the approach it advocates is essentially the same as I suggest in this book.

## Commentary

In the chapters that follow, we will consider each of the elements and major activities of an internal audit department that audits what matters to its stakeholders. As a result, the function itself is seen as having great value, helping the board and executive management deliver success and value to its stakeholders.

When internal audit speaks, people listen because what it says matters to them.

## Chapter 2: The risks that matter

How often does an audit report get the attention of the full board?

Rarely, if ever.

Most of the time, the audit committee is the final destination of audit communications; it is very unusual for an audit report to merit a spot on the agenda of the full board.

It may be that these audit reports matter to the audit committee. But, do they matter in the grand scheme of things? Do they, and should they, matter to the full board or executive management committee?

Do the issues typically identified by internal audit lead to actions by the board or top management, such as a shift in strategy?

Does the board look for assurance from internal audit before endorsing management proposals for new initiatives?

Is the New Zealand director right when he says that "Almost all of IA findings are mundane operational compliance issues"? How often has a company failed as a result of deficiencies in accounts payable? Yet, this is an annual audit in many companies[5].

What are these "critical risks to the enterprise" that KPMG refers to, and why is internal audit at the majority of organizations failing to address them?

I have worked at quite a few organizations as an internal audit manager and then CAE. Let me talk about the most critical risk areas at some of them.

---

[5] On rare occasions, accounts payable and even travel and expense reporting may be sources of significant risk. For example, a professional services firm may see significant sources of risk to its objectives in travel and expense reporting.

Home Savings of America

My first internal audit positions, where I ran part of the department, were at Di Giorgio Corporation (a $2bn conglomerate) and Home Savings of America (the largest savings and loan association in the U.S., similar in operations and size to a mid-size bank). In both, internal audit performed what I would call traditional audits. We focused on risks that were important to operating management, but I would not say that we were addressing the most critical risks to the organization's success.

For example, and this is much clearer in hindsight, Home Savings' success hinged on four issues:

a. its ability to attract its target customer base of older, more affluent citizens;

b. its ability to grow and then to maintain an asset size that would allow it to compete with the banks;

c. whether its computer systems would provide its customers with the experience they desired; and,

d. its ability to keep operating expenses low.

The Home Savings internal audit never really addressed any of these critical areas. It played around the edges.

For example, we never looked at risks relating to customer satisfaction; the selection of acquisition targets or the success of the transitions after acquisition; the ability of the IT function to innovate; or how management managed cost.

While my team and I performed an operational audit of IT that focused on service to *internal* customers, we never considered its competitive edge when it came to its *real* customers – the holders of checking and savings accounts, mortgage loans, etc.

Internal audit was not seen as critical to the company, perhaps illustrated by the CAE not being a senior vice president and only reporting to an executive three levels below the CEO.

Home Savings was acquired about 10 years after I left. It had not been able to keep up with its competitors in terms of growth, profitability, or computer systems. Should internal audit have helped avoid this fate? Perhaps it should have done more to highlight its core weaknesses.

## Tosco Corporation

My next internal audit role was with Tosco, where I was privileged to work for ten years. During that time, the company grew from $2bn to $28bn in revenue and my team grew from four (including me) to more than fifty.

In the early days, the company operated a single refinery (the Avon refinery in Martinez, California) and a phosphate fertilizer mining company in central Florida. The Avon refinery represented by far the greater source of revenue (and, most of the time, profits) and also by far the greater source of potential harm from safety and other risks.

When I joined the company in 1990, it had just moved its operations from Santa Monica and Bakersfield in Southern California to Concord in Northern California. It had lost quite a few key accounting and IT personnel and when I built the audit plan I took that into account. The risk of an error in accounting, not only in terms of external financial reporting to the SEC but also in its management reporting, was high. But, my small staff of three and I spent the majority of our time looking at Avon operations.

While financial reporting was important, it was unlikely to bring the company to its knees. However, compliance with safety and environmental laws and regulations was critical beyond compliance and reputation risk; a failure could lead not only to loss of life[6] but also to the regulators making us cease operations – and pay a fine which, frankly, we could not afford. Tosco was also paying millions of dollars to acquire crude oil as feedstock for Avon, and periodic major maintenance (referred to as 'turnarounds') cost about a million dollars a day. Failures to manage those costs would probably lead to the failure of the company.

---

[6] This was very dear to the heart of the refinery management, including myself and the audit team, as our offices were within the refinery.

As we performed these audit engagements at Avon, we found many deficiencies – too many to indicate other than a significant problem. In fact, the problem (or should I say, problems) ran deep. For example, when we attended safety training (mandatory for all employees and contractors who worked in the refinery), we saw trainers helping some of the contractors' staff. Apparently, some of these individuals had a problem retaining the instructions. So, perhaps out of impatience, Avon staff members were helping them answer and pass the tests required to be certified to work.

This might be considered a *culture* problem. Safety was taken seriously by senior management (every senior staff meeting opened with a safety briefing and any incidents were discussed in depth), but clearly not by supervisors and staff.

We also found that the direct reports to the Avon refinery manager not only disliked and had little respect for each other, but competed, didn't share information, and often were unable to work in a collaborative fashion. But while these senior managers had little respect for each other, they had even less respect for their boss. The Avon management team was quite dysfunctional.

Our audit reports helped Tosco executive management see the extent of the problem.

At the end of each year, I provided the audit committee and top management a formal report with my assessment of the system of internal controls. Back then (1990-1992), we were not talking about risk management; in my report, I said that the assessment was of internal controls over the more significant risks.

In the early years, my annual reports always indicated that controls at Avon were deficient and the risks were high. When I discussed the assessment with the audit committee and top management, I shared my concerns about the ability of the Avon management team to change the situation.

It was not long before senior management decided to make a change, replacing the Avon refinery manager. He was an excellent technician but a poor manager and team leader.

I met with the new refinery manager before he started (by then, we had acquired another refinery that he was managing) and made sure he knew of my concerns. But, what he found when he started still surprised him, and it was not long before he was in my office asking for internal audit's help. He said that if we only continued with traditional audits, which he recognized were appropriate and necessary because of the risk level, all we would do was "add to my to-do list". He asked instead if we could find a way to help him complete the actions *already* on that long list.

My team and I discussed this and our first step was to prioritize all our existing, open audit findings. This helped him prioritize related work. We then decided which audit engagements were likely to identify *significant* additional issues meriting his attention; others were postponed to the next year.

In time, the new Avon management team made significant improvements in operations.

The audit team adapted to the changed risk landscape. We still performed audits to ensure that controls over safety and environmental compliance risks were in place; but we placed an increased level of focus on cost control – now the most significant area of risk for this low margin business.

In the meantime, Tosco had made a number of significant acquisitions and its revenue (and profits) continued to grow at a steady pace. One of the first acquisitions was of a major refinery and related businesses (pipelines and wholesale terminals) in New Jersey.

The Bayway refinery, which was purchased from ExxonMobil, doubled the size of the company. Located on New York harbor, Bayway offered multiple opportunities. The U.S. East Coast market tended to operate counter-cyclically to the West Coast, where Avon was located. Now Tosco had operations of roughly similar size on each coast, and this tended to smooth out earnings fluctuations. (The phosphate fertilizer company was sold around this time.)

The investors responded very positively because now our earnings were far more predictable[7]. When Tosco relied on Avon alone, the cyclical nature of the West Coast market led to huge swings from year to year. Several years of healthy profits might be followed by a year or two of significant losses. Now, Tosco was fairly steadily profitable.

Another opportunity was presented because New York harbor was the delivery point for crude oil futures traded on the New York Mercantile Exchange (NYMEX). Bayway was the only refinery that was actually on that harbor, so it presented a natural "hedge" opportunity. Let me explain.

Tosco could acquire a derivatives contract on NYMEX for delivery of a defined quantity of crude oil (West Texas Intermediate, or WTI) on a defined date. The contract would 'lock in' the purchase price for that future purchase, avoiding the risk of price fluctuation. Tosco could also purchase a contract to sell the gasoline and other refined products that it would manufacture from that crude oil. In that way, it would lock in the margin, the level of gross profit, it would obtain. Rather than being subject to the vagaries of the market, which could fluctuate significantly from day to day, Tosco could guarantee a defined level of profit for the majority of Bayway's production.

With this in mind, Tosco built a derivatives trading operation. It had a small team supporting Avon's crude oil purchasing needs and selling much of its refined products. But now it needed a much larger and more sophisticated capability to take advantage of NYMEX-traded futures contracts and options as well as over-the-counter trades with other companies and financial institutions. The trading team engaged in hundreds of millions of dollars of trades to hedge its commodity risk. One of the traders was authorized to make speculative trades, within limits.

The trading operation represented a significant risk and a concern to the audit committee. Even though I engaged an external consultant with significant commodities trading experience to support our audits, the

---

[7] It is important for internal audit to understand not only the objectives of the organization but its value drivers. Discussions with the group responsible for investor relations can be fruitful.

audit committee insisted that I, as CAE, obtain personal training in derivatives trading so that I would understand the mechanics as well as the big picture. I attended a two-week class in New York; although most of it was over my head, I grasped enough to understand the principles, basic mechanics, risks, and key controls necessary to manage derivatives trading.

We audited the trading operation every quarter for the first year and more. It was necessary as the initial processes, systems, controls, and oversight were immature. As they matured, the level of risk came down, but still remained one of the higher risks to the organization, meriting formal audits each year and monitoring on a monthly basis. (I received copies of reports sent to management so I could see the level of trading, open positions, and results.)

A failure in controls led to a situation that, in hindsight, is amusing. This is how I described it in *World-Class Internal Auditing: Tales from my Journey.*

> I was visiting my team and management of a major business unit in the US when I heard that the unit's CEO was running around the building, angry and anxious. Apparently, one of our accounting groups had processed an invoice against the counterparty to a derivatives trade that was not only wrong but absurdly wrong.
>
> The company was a very active user of derivatives transactions to hedge the prices of its raw materials and finished products. On occasion, it entered into "swap" trades with counterparties in the business or with financial institutions. In these trades, one company would agree to purchase quantities of one product and sell quantities of another to the other party at a certain date. Initially, the value of each of the two transactions would be the same. The market prices would fluctuate and when the agreed date arrived, one party would owe the other a (typically) small amount – the difference between the value from the sale and the cost of the purchase. However, on this occasion our accounting group sent the counterparty an invoice for the full amount of the sale side of the swap, not the difference.

19

Our CEO was running around looking for a two *billion* dollar invoice! He ran from accounting to IT to the room with the printers to the mail room. Eventually it was found, fortunately before it was mailed to the counterparty and our reputation damaged.

The book goes on to explain the root cause of the error – a leadership failure by the manager responsible for the commercial accounting function.

As you might expect, as the company grew and its systems, processes, and organization matured, its risk profile changed.

In fact, the changes in systems and processes were the source of the most significant risks! I am a strong believer that the source of many significant risks can usually be found where there is change.

At Tosco, IT auditors always represented a significant proportion of my audit team. Commentators today, in 2016, talk about how technology is critical to the success of any organization. I can tell you that was also the case in 1990 at Tosco and in the mid-1980's at Home Savings! Computer systems were not only how we ran the accounting and related activities of the company, but most of the refinery's operations were highly automated. The temperature, pressure, and flow rates in the refinery's processing units were all controlled by automated systems.

My initial team in 1990 consisted of two financial/operational auditors and one IT auditor. As the company and internal audit grew, I maintained about the same proportion of IT auditors. They were occasionally supplemented by co-sourced specialists, primarily from Arthur Andersen and its successor, Protiviti. In fact, it was an Arthur Andersen 'white hat' penetration testing team that demonstrated that our information security was so weak that they were able to attain 'root level' access to some of the refinery systems. This was a huge risk, as a hacker could change temperature or pressure levels and cause a refinery unit to catch fire or explode – likely causing severe injuries or death to operating staff. Even then, we were well aware that our nation's infrastructure was vulnerable to attack!

Information security was important and received a fair level of attention from the team. But, the likelihood of a major failure was not high. The greater risk was that a failure to manage the tens of millions the company was investing in new systems, such as a new financial system and (later) ERP, would lead to serious process failures affecting our ability to bill customers, pay bills, provide management with operating information, and file reliable financial statements.

I was quick to dedicate a serious part of the internal audit team to participate in systems implementations. I say "participate" because I didn't see internal audit as an 'auditor' per se. Our role was not to find the issues and then toss them over the wall for management to address. Rather, I told my team that I would assess our involvement as a success or failure, not by the quantity or severity of issues we identified and reported, but by the success of the implementation.

If we reported serious issues and management did not buy into taking corrective actions, I would call that a failure[8].

If we reported serious issues that were fixed, but we missed other issues that caused the project to fail, I would call that a failure of ours as well.

Our interests were aligned with those of management – we needed the systems implementation project to succeed.

I consider this 'proactive' auditing. The best assurance that controls will be adequate is if issues are detected and corrected prior to implementation.

I started this approach when I was with Home Savings. My intent was to issue a report to management (usually the project oversight team, a mix of IT and user management) prior to systems go-live. The report would provide our assessment, our opinion, that if the system was implemented as designed (and tested), the controls should be adequate. This required that we identify design, testing, or implementation issues early and work collaboratively with management to ensure appropriate action was taken before go-live.

In Chapter 1, I mentioned a systems implementation at Tosco where the users and IT management had a heated argument about who was to

---

[8] See *Findings and Recommendations* in Chapter 12.

blame for problems with a systems implementation and the CFO looked to the internal audit lead for an objective perspective. I had assigned my top two direct reports, an IT audit manager and a financial/operational audit manager with decades of experience in refining operations, to the project. They were able to provide the CFO, CIO, and executive management with objective and informed *insight*[9] into not only what was wrong but why and how the issues had occurred. In fact, both sides were at fault (IT more than the users).

Years later, Tosco's Marketing Company had a major systems implementation project that nearly went seriously sideways and could have led to massive operating difficulties for the division – which represented about 35% of the company's revenues. This is how I described it in *World-Class Internal Auditing: Tales from my Journey*:

> The company owned about 6,000 stores across the United States and did not believe its current systems would be able to continue to support the business.

> The IT department worked with management of store operations and related departments in a disciplined process to identify their needs and select a solution they believed offered the best long-term capabilities.

> When the project was given the go-ahead from executive management, together with a budget in excess of a million dollars for hardware, software, and consultants from Accenture, I again assigned some of my best people. Three IT audit managers (Tim Cox, Bruce Taylor, and Will Helton) were joined by an experienced audit manager (Jennifer Busch) with a business and financial focus.

> They soon came to my office with shell-shock in their faces.

> They asked me whether I knew what solutions the project team had selected. I didn't, so they told me.

---

[9] The IIA published Core Principles for effective internal auditing in 2015. The abilities to provide insight and to be forward-looking, both of which were evident during this project, are key capabilities for an internal audit department that produces work that matters.

The company was going to replace all the systems in the individual convenience stores. These ran the sales registers, maintained inventory and other records, and once or more each day uploaded information to the central system in our Phoenix data center. Both the hardware and the software were going to be replaced.

The software was designed for and used only by clothing boutiques in shopping malls. It had never been used in convenience stores.

It was going to run on hardware that it had never run on, and which also had never been used in a convenience store business.

There was no evidence, at least not to my team's satisfaction, that the hardware and software would work well together and be able to handle the volume in a typical convenience store.

As if this was not enough, the central system that collected data from the stores, was used by our Stores Accounting staff to run reports analyzing the business, and then fed the financial and other enterprise applications, was also being replaced. This time, the software was one that had been used in a convenience store business but the hardware on which it was going to run had not – and the software had never run on that hardware.

The central system had never worked with the new store systems, of course.

As you can imagine, the audit team was very concerned. They believed, with every justification, that this was a project with a high risk of failure. Such a failure could have a massive effect on our business, effectively closing down our stores if things went badly.

I gave them my speech about their success being intertwined with the success of the project, and this was an opportunity to be of huge value to the company. They probably muttered to themselves about their mad manager, but they left determined and resolute.

During the course of the project, I was able to hire a highly technical IT auditor, Alan Proctor. This was fortunate as the project team had decided they needed to upgrade the security side of the central system. Alan not only provided technical insights they could use on the alternatives (he knew them, they didn't) but was also able to steer them in the right direction to avoid some of the potential security loopholes.

As the go-live date neared, my team asked to meet with me and discuss the situation.

Tim and Bruce spoke for the team when they said that there was a high risk that something would crash. It wasn't just a matter of controls and security. The size and scope of the entire system, when you consider the number of stores, the volume of transactions, and the fact that everything was new and the pieces had never been used in combination, was very complex.

The project team had not been able to test everything working together with anything like the volume of transactions that could be anticipated upon go-live.

Tim and Bruce believed that management should be informed that going live without additional testing in an environment more consistent with go-live conditions (i.e., with more realistic volumes) was high risk – in their view, unacceptably high risk.

I encouraged them to share this at the upcoming project steering committee meeting, when the CFO and CIO would be present. After they left, I made sure that the CFO and CIO knew that we had an important message to share and that the team would have sufficient time on the agenda.

I didn't attend the meeting myself (I trusted my team and had other serious matters to attend to), but my team did well. They informed me that top management had listened carefully; they had asked questions of the project team who had confirmed the facts upon which Tim, Bruce, and the others had based their assessment.

However, they considered not only the risk and cost of going forward with the implementation without delay, but the risk and cost of a postponement while they performed additional testing. Apparently, it would take some extended period of time for them to design a test environment with similar volumes as the live environment. In addition, they would have to extend any delay until after the year-end close – which would result in the loss of key consultants from Accenture.

The CFO and CIO decided to take the risk and forge ahead.

My team was downcast. However, we talked about what we could do to reduce the risk of a devastating crash and/or mitigate any damage.

They decided that they could identify the areas where the system was most likely to crash.

Brilliant! To this day, I am proud of this imaginative solution.

The team met with senior IT and project management to discuss which areas were most at risk. IT and users put people in place to monitor each of these high risk areas, with instructions on what to do should they fail.

As it happened, the new system failed in several areas – all of which had been predicted by the team! The prompt actions by the people watching these areas mitigated the damage to the extent that it was barely noticeable.

The overall project manager came into my office to tell me how grateful he was to everybody on the team, and to me for making them not only available but willing to do whatever they could to help the project succeed.

He was followed by the CIO. He told me that he would never again implement a major new system without first obtaining an assessment and advice from my team of IT auditors.

I will have more to share about my time with Tosco in later chapters. But I mentioned one area of risk earlier that merits mention now.

Both the Refining and Marketing arms of the company needed to manage their expenditures with great care. For example, the refineries (of which Tosco owned nine by 2001) spent massive amounts of money on 'turnarounds'. This is where the refinery would shut down one or more of its units for periodic maintenance. The company would spend a million dollars or more *per day* for contractors to come in and service the unit. Although every effort was made to time the turnaround such that revenues were only marginally impacted, refinery production could be significantly reduced.

From an internal audit point of view, management's ability to manage these turnarounds merited a priority positioning in our audit plan. But, I didn't think that was enough.

We had the capability to audit these contractors and ensure that they complied with the provisions of our contracts with them. With the approval of the audit committee, I was able to obtain a budget and establish a Contracts Audit team that delivered significant value, saving the company several million each year[10].

## Solectron

I left Tosco when the company was sold to Phillips Petroleum and I joined Solectron Corporation.

Solectron was a contracts manufacturer for electronics companies, manufacturing or assembling mobile phones, computers, digital switches, and more for major global companies. It dominated the market for outsourced electronics manufacturing when I joined in 2001 (revenues were approximately $16bn), and had a storied history of entrepreneurship, innovation, and customer service. In fact, it was the first company to win two Malcom Baldridge awards for quality.

---

[10] Under the initial leadership of contracts audit maestro/guru Bill Baker and then Connie Chapman, the Contracts Audit team delivered a consistent ROI of about 12:1, even as it grew from a single individual to more than 20. They delivered millions in cost-savings, to the extent that one year the CFO of the Marketing company put their cost recoveries on a separate line in the management financial reports discussed at the executive annual off-site because, in his words, "they distorted the results for the year".

What I didn't realize until after I had settled into my new position as Vice President, Internal Audit, was that this was a company in trouble.

The CEO, Ko Nishimura, was one of the reasons I joined the company. A story I heard about him was about a customer who called to complain about delays in the delivery of products we had manufactured. Rather than tasking a subordinate to take action, Ko personally went down to the factory, loaded the parts into his personal vehicle, and drove them to the customer himself. I found Ko to be passionate, curious, and a fascinating individual.

However fascinating and inspiring he was to me, he was not motivating to his management team. He wanted to delegate authority to his direct reports. However, he had given them too much authority and power. Not only did they resist instructions from him, but they went so far as to show disrespect to him in executive meetings and even with the board.

The company had become highly fragmented. Executives in charge of geographical regions and business units went their own way with little regard for the corporation as a whole. For example, each implemented their choice of computer systems so we had multiple solutions for each problem. The managers in charge of accounting and information systems at each location reported to the general manager for that area or business unit, not to the corporate CFO or CIO.

The greatest risk to the company lay in this management and organizational structure dysfunction.

Within a very short time, the board acted. It replaced both the CEO and the CFO. However, the replacements were not a panacea.

I heard from several executives (I did not witness this myself) that the new CEO frequently challenged two or more executives to propose a solution to a problem. This created a competitive environment that in turn led to the executives keeping information to themselves and otherwise failing to act as a team. I also heard that the CEO rarely listened to his direct reports and was seen by some as a 'bully'.

As an example, at one point the company acquired a successful and rapidly growing company in New England. It operated customer call centers and technical help desk services for major organizations. But, there was no provision in the contract to retain any of the top executives and none of the Solectron executives wanted to take control. The business faltered and faded until it was sold for pennies on the dollar.

Another example is an even more striking of the effect of the management team dysfunction. A year or so after he joined the company, the new CEO visited the company's factory in Guadalajara, Mexico. The company had previously invested in an extension to the factory, but until now it had been empty (a problem I will address in a moment). The CEO was pleased to hear that a major new contract with a Canadian telecommunications company would make productive use of the empty space. He asked for details of the contract and was told that the deal would provide a single digit *gross* margin (i.e., before overhead expenses). There was more: management had been forced to agree to substantial price reductions in each of the remaining years of the contract. Why, the CEO asked, did you agree to such disadvantageous terms, which might not even result in a profit? He was told that the competition had been fierce. When he asked which of our competitors had been involved, he was informed that it was our own factory in Suzhou, China!

Even in the face of such information about the effects of the fragmented organization, little change was made. One of the reasons was that the fragmented IT environment provided very little insight into the condition of operations across the more than 100 factories spread across the globe. (Another was that each regional executive protected their operations.)

What we did know was that most of our factories were operating at less than 60% capacity. In other words, 40% or more of the equipment and space was idle or, at best, under-utilized. This drove up unit costs, a problem for the long-term future of the company.

As the CAE, I was faced with multiple problems. The internal audit department I inherited had many excellent features, including some talented people, the respect of the audit committee, and a reasonable audit reporting structure.

However, it was performing only a small number of audits each year, doing what we might call 'full scope' audits of the larger factories. While these few factories were significantly larger than the others, Solectron's profit margins were so small that issues at a handful of the small locations could be material to the company as a whole.

In addition, internal audit was not performing any audits of the corporate functions – or of the management of common functions across the organization.

As I had at Tosco, I wanted to provide the audit committee and top management with a formal assessment each year on the internal controls over the more significant risks to the organization.

I needed to change the audit approach from a few micro-level audits of risks to individual locations to multiple audits of risks to the enterprise as a whole. That required:

    a. Identifying the more significant risks to the company as a whole

    b. Understanding the sources of those risks – where the issues were most likely to arise – and building the audit plan to address them

    c. Changing the audit organization from one where a large team (of as many as half the audit department) performed a full scope audit, to one where one or two people could complete an audit focused on a few risks

    d. Implementing an audit approach that enabled remote reviews of risks at smaller locations and on-site reviews where the risk merited

    e. Changing the audit reporting process to make it easier to consume for the executives and the board

I am going to discuss in the next chapter how I go about identifying the risks that matter, so I will leave that process for the moment. But, it was clear that apart from the underlying issue of dysfunctional corporate management and a fragmented organization, the more significant areas of risk were:

    ❑ The procurement of quality materials, delivered promptly and reliably, at a reasonable price

- ❏ The negotiation of advantageous sales contracts, especially when manufacturing was performed at multiple factories in different regions

- ❏ The manufacturing of quality products that satisfied the customer and were delivered on time according to the contract

- ❏ Manufacturing utilization and capacity planning in general

- ❏ The provision of information to corporate and business unit executive management, enabling effective decision-making

The audits we performed to address each risk area included audits of corporate-wide processes (where they existed) and related processes at selected sites.

For example, the audit plan included a combination of audits to address materials procurement risk. The combination was necessary as each location did its own procurement; sometimes they utilized corporate purchase agreements, but not always. I decided that the best approach would be to staff the audit with my most senior people: the internal audit directors[11] for Americas and Asia/Pacific, and my contracts audit manager.

- ❏ The first step was to obtain an understanding of the corporate contracting process (which covered a limited number of purchased components) and the monitoring by the corporate Chief Procurement Officer.

- ❏ Then the team visited, in turn, the locations I had selected for an on-site audit: the two largest in Asia (which included the site that appeared to have the most effective procurement function), the location in the Americas that had the best reputation, and the largest site in Europe.

- ❏ Then, the team sat back and assessed how effective procurement of materials was overall – looking at the organization as a whole.

---

[11] Shelly Hobbs and Audrey Lee

Our report assessed the overall effectiveness of procurement as an opportunity for improvement that could be material to the profitability of the company. We pointed out that the Penang, Malaysia operation was best-in-class. The fact that they were frequently able to obtain better prices when negotiating just for Penang than the corporate function had been able to negotiate for the whole company was not only a concern but pointed to an opportunity.

Our report mattered.

We performed similar audit engagements for the other more significant risks.

I left the company after only three years. Frankly, while I felt that I had made major upgrades to the effectiveness of the internal audit department and received commendations from the audit committee, the board and top management had not been able to make the radical changes necessary for long-term success. I had made sure they were aware of the challenges and actively supported the initiatives that were intended to address them (such as one to rationalize the footprint, close sites, and improve capacity utilization). However, even the initiatives they started never got full executive support and floundered. By the time I left, revenues were on the decline (as our competitors and their lower cost structure outbid us for new contracts) and within a few years the company was sold to a rival.

### Maxtor

Maxtor was a completely different story. A manufacturer of hard disk drives with revenues of about $4bn, I was hired to run internal audit and the Sarbanes-Oxley (SOX) compliance program, and to help them improve related business processes.

Initially, I was hired as a consultant on their SOX program while they obtained approval for a vice president position. This was a program in trouble: they had a number of material weaknesses and significant deficiencies and had restated their financial reports several times (they had actually restated every filing with the Securities and Exchange

Commission except the proxy statement). It was clear that the only path to success would involve some process redesign and upgrade, so I asked for and received the position description of Vice President, Process and Controls Assurance. I reported to the audit committee of the board for the internal audit role, to the CFO for SOX, and to the CEO for process consulting work.

The internal audit and SOX work had been outsourced to KPMG. I was able to bring that work in-house and build a team of experienced and highly talented individuals based in California, Colorado, and Singapore.

The first task was to help the company upgrade the finance function. At my first audit committee meeting, I had the dubious honor of explaining to the board members and top management that there was a potential material weakness in the system of internal control over financial reporting that had not previously been shared with them: nobody in the corporate financial reporting function was a CPA or equivalent. In fact, the only CPAs in the corporate office were the Treasurer, a business unit controller, and me. Historically, the company had placed too much reliance on the external auditors (PwC) and this was not only no longer permissible but meant that there was an unacceptable risk of an error due to misunderstanding accounting rules and interpretations – in other words, a potential material weakness.

The audit committee asked for action and it was swiftly taken. The company hired a new Corporate Controller and brought in an experienced CFO.

We made excellent progress in the first year. When we made our end of year assessment of internal control, it was clean: no material weaknesses or significant deficiencies.

We had also completed a number of internal audits, both assurance and consulting engagements. The more significant risk areas included:

❑ New product development

❑ Component material cost

❑ Product quality

While the company was a market leader, the technology in hard drives was advancing significantly. Smaller drives were constantly being developed, with increased capacity. However, our research and development staff was struggling to come up with products that met these requirements at an acceptable cost – hence the second area of risk listed above. This was a risk well known to the board and top management. In fact, the board insisted that the CEO replace the head of the R&D department; when he refused, both the CEO and the R&D head were fired!

The new CEO (the former chair of the board, who had served as CEO some years earlier) and head of R&D were excellent. But, the change was not enough.

The core component of every Maxtor hard drive was expensive – far more expensive than the equivalent component in our competitors' drives. The company had built a specialized factory to manufacture up to 40% of its requirements, but that factory was in California while our competitors had built their factories in China. The balance of 60% or more was purchased from a vendor in Taiwan. That vendor was the only one capable of supplying the component to our specifications, but Maxtor was not a major customer. It had several much larger customers and when they increased their order level, we were often put on 'allocation'; in other words, we were only provided a percentage of our requirements, limiting our own manufacturing capability. Further, we had no real leverage in negotiating prices with the vendor and we were forced to pay premium prices – again, far in excess of our competitors' costs.

There was little any internal audit function could do about either of these top two risks. We did audit the company's California factory and helped identify a few savings opportunities, but that was never going to be enough. We gave moral encouragement to the company's initiative to build a new factory in Thailand.

Before closing the loop on that, let me tackle the third risk area on the list above.

Competition was fierce and we could not afford any product quality issues. We performed audits of the product quality processes, including an audit at our largest factory (in Suzhou, China) that looked at what appeared to be a high level of scrap. Obviously, high levels of scrap could be an indicator of potential quality issues as well as increased levels of cost. All of this mattered to the success of the company.

Coming back to the issue of cost, which exacerbated our inability to develop cost-effective new products, management was forced to cancel several development projects that were not succeeding fast enough. Instead, they focused all efforts on one or two initiatives.

But even that was not enough. The die was cast. The company was going to be overtaken in the market and we could already see revenues falling and the bottom line was turning bright red.

A major competitor made an offer to acquire the company and the board accepted it.

Internal audit and our colleagues in Finance had excelled, but the patient had died. It was time to move on again.

## Business Objects

Business Objects was a software company, the leader in the business intelligence or analytics market, with about $1.25bn in revenues. As a result, almost all its risks of significance related to the sales cycle.

The external auditor, Ernst & Young (EY), often told the audit committee that the top risks when it came to financial reporting were revenue recognition, revenue recognition, and revenue recognition. They spent the majority of their time in that area, and the sales cycle in general was where we spent much of our time in internal audit.

Revenue recognition is a complex area, with many opportunities to get the accounting wrong and materially misstate the financial statements. Fortunately, the company had significant expertise among its finance staff and legal personnel and errors were rare.

One risk was fraud. In fact, the year prior to my joining the company, a series of frauds (apparently unrelated) had been uncovered in Asia. A team of internal and external auditors had found revenue-related fraud in several countries in the region, and this led to the dismissal of multiple regional executives, including finance personnel.

We performed a risk assessment and put monitoring in place using the company's own software for the more significant and likely fraud schemes. These involved an employee (sometimes multiple employees were involved) agreeing with either a customer or a channel partner (somebody that would act as an agent for us) to inflate sales in one quarter and write a credit note in the next quarter. The inflated sales would, in turn, inflate the employee commissions and bonuses. Our monitoring looked for spikes in credit notes in the first six weeks of a quarter.

Fraud investigations consumed a fair amount of my time, especially when a senior individual was involved.

But there were other risks that we focused on in the audit plan.

A couple of risks related to key personnel having the ability to perform the careful review of sales contracts necessary to protect the company – from bad deals as well to ensure revenue recognition requirements were met.

One audit focused on the legal personnel that supported the UK and other European sales groups. I had heard from some of them that they were understaffed and I knew that some executives were looking outside the company for legal assistance – or forgoing legal advice, which was an even greater risk.

My team (based in Paris) looked at the hours that Legal spent reviewing contracts of various size and complexity. They developed analytics with Business Objects software to understand what was happening and found that Legal spent about the same time on small, simple contracts as they spent on larger, more complex contracts. The team didn't stop there. Their analysis helped them determine at what break point, at what size of contract, the company should allow the legal review to be shorter – because the risk was lower. The audit recommendations ensured every contract had an appropriate level of review and there was no longer a need for executives to go outside the company for legal advice.

Another risk that surfaced (especially after the sale of the company to SAP was announced) was that we would lose key personnel involved in the sales contract review process: finance, legal, or credit personnel.

Again, we developed monitoring software to alert us when key personnel gave their notice; we used this to follow-up with management and confirm that they had the risk adequately addressed.

An interesting audit involved the discounts that the company offered customers. They amounted to hundreds of millions of dollars, a very significant percentage of the company's revenues. Our audit not only identified that the company's approval policy (for example, that all discounts over a certain level had to be approved by an executive vice president) was not being followed and that management had no way to know when the policy was not being followed, but that at least one senior executive was deliberately reporting a lower level of discount on a major deal so that it would be approved. Sales executives were being compensated based on revenue, not profit – a common weakness of sales commission and bonus policies (i.e., not limited to Business Objects or even to the software industry). The executive was discounting a major deal to an unacceptably low level because he knew that was necessary to make the sale. If the correct discount level had been reported, management would not have approved the contract – and the executive would not have received the commission. The executive was terminated.

However, the greatest risk was competitor-related. We were not particularly concerned that our competitors would bring to market software products that surpassed ours. Management and the board felt that we had a significant edge in that regard. But, major software companies (such as Microsoft, IBM, Oracle, and SAP who were several times our size) were showing a lot of interest in acquiring a business intelligence company. If they acquired one of our competitors, they could bring a lot of marketing muscle and influence that would strengthen that competitor in the market place – especially if they integrated the business intelligence products into their own.

By now, I was acting as the risk officer for the company as well as CAE. I knew that the management team was carefully monitoring what was happening with our competitors and the major software vendors. Internal audit was not going to add anything of value by performing an engagement that focused on competitive risk.

Even though this was a major risk area for the company, there was little value in auditing how management was addressing it.

In the end, IBM and Oracle acquired the second and third largest of our competitors, and the board agreed to let Business Objects be acquired by SAP.

## Commentary

What I have attempted to describe above is how the risks that mattered to each company not only varied from company to company, but from time to time.

What matters to a company in 2015 is not necessarily the same as what matters in 2016.

What matters to one company may be different to what matters to its closest competitor.

Have I ever performed audits of areas that don't really matter to the board and top management? Yes, but only one time.

At Tosco, for example, when I joined the company the financial people and systems had just moved from Bakersfield and Santa Monica to Concord. Several people, both at manager and staff level, were new. I needed to gain assurance that the basic systems were in decent shape before channeling all resources to those that were critical to survival.

After that, whether at Tosco, Solectron, Maxtor, or Business Objects, we only audited areas like accounts payable and payroll for SOX compliance. While there are risks in these areas, they were not sufficiently high to merit inclusion in the audit plan. Even if there was a failure in controls, which we assessed as unlikely, the impact on the organization would not be high.

Some pore over the list of 'top risks' that consultants and others publish from time to time. While these are interesting and merit consideration, they may be quite different from what the board and top management – and internal audit – have to manage to enable the organization to succeed.

Internal audit needs to understand which risks matter and then determine what they can and should do about those risks. But, first, I want to discuss some of the methods internal audit can use to identify which risks matter to the enterprise.

## Chapter 3: Knowing which risks matter

*In an ideal world*, it is easy to know which risks matter to the success of the organization.

### Key Risks Disclosures

*In an ideal world*, the most significant risks are disclosed to investors and regulators in the company's filings (in a Key Risks section, or equivalent[12]). However, most organizations include an exhaustive list[13] of risks in their filings without distinguishing which are believed to be most likely or which are being monitored most closely by management and the board. Still, the Key Risks section of the regulatory findings is an important source of information and internal auditors should consider everything listed there.

It is important to note that the regulatory filings contain a list of risks *at a point in time* and may not include all risks to the success of the organization that management must address as they run the organization every day and with which internal audit might be concerned. I will discuss this in a bit.

### Reliance on the ERM program

*In an ideal world*, the company would have an enterprise-wide risk management program (ERM) that can be relied upon for a list of the risks

---

[12] Some refer to this section as 'Risk Factors', and the rules about the disclosure of risks in filings with the regulators vary from country to country.

[13] *Exhausting* may be the better term for a list that consumes many pages of text but often provides investors with scant information on which risks the board is most concerned about. A *kitchen sink* approach leads organizations to list everything they can think of, even if they are not on the board's radar, in case they occur and lead to a drop in share value. At the same time, organizations are loath to provide risk information that would help their competitors – leading to an exhausting list with little useful and actionable information.

that matter. However, in the real world the ERM program may be less than ideal.

As with the regulatory disclosure, the majority of ERM programs only provide a list of risks that is updated and reviewed on a periodic basis. Sometimes, that period may be as long as 3-6 months, or even a year. I have run into ERM programs where a list of risks is only reviewed every two years!

Internal audit needs to focus on the risks that matter *now* and will matter over the *next year or so*.

I like to quote Wayne Gretzky. The famous ice hockey player was once asked what the secret his success was. He replied that his father had taught him to "skate to where the puck is *going to be*."

In the same way, internal audit needs to be concerned about the risks to the organization's current objectives and what they will face over the next 12-18 months. History is just that – history.

Note: this is different from the current practice of many organizations, where internal audit focuses on the risks that it has seen in the past year, perhaps what is considered a current risk, but not what will concern the organization over the next year.

In the Introduction, I referenced the 2015 *Core Principles for Effective Internal Audit*. They include this, that internal audit should:

Be insightful, proactive, and future-focused.

Risks do not wait for a periodic review to change. As I said in *World-Class Risk Management*, risk is dynamic. It is changed or created with every decision. Internal audit cannot rely on a list of risks that used to be present. It needs to have a list of current and future[14] risks.

Before internal audit can rely on a list of risks provided by the company's ERM program, it has to confirm that the said ERM program can be relied upon and is current.

---

[14] I suggest a timeline of 12-18 months.

The *International Standards for the Professional Practice of Internal Auditing*[15] (*Standards*) include this:

> **Standard 2120**: the internal audit activity must evaluate the effectiveness and contribute to the improvement of risk management processes.
>
> **Interpretation**: Determining whether risk management processes are effective is a judgment resulting from the internal auditor's assessment that:
>
> - Organizational objectives support and align with the organization's mission;
>
> - Significant risks are identified and assessed;
>
> - Appropriate risk responses are selected that align risks with the organization's risk appetite; and
>
> - Relevant risk information is captured and communicated in a timely manner across the organization, enabling staff, management, and the board to carry out their responsibilities.
>
> - The internal audit activity may gather the information to support this assessment during multiple engagements. The results of these engagements, when viewed together,

---

[15] The IIA though their Standards Board maintain and publish the *Standards* as part of the *International Professional Practices Framework* that also includes the *Core Principles for the Professional Practice of Internal Auditing*, the *Definition of Internal Auditing*, and the *Code of Ethics*.

Excerpts from the *Standards* and other IIA materials are included in this book by permission of The Institute of Internal Auditors, Inc.© 2016 by The Institute of Internal Auditors, Inc.

The Excerpts are current as of October 1st, 2016. The IIA routinely updates their guidance.

provide an understanding of the organization's risk management processes and their effectiveness. Risk management processes are monitored through ongoing management activities, separate evaluations, or both.

All of this is useful and I recommend the IIA's Practice Guide *Assessing the Adequacy of Risk Management using ISO 31000*.

However, for purposes of knowing whether the ERM program can be relied upon by internal audit, I would ask these questions:

- ❑ Does the ERM program provide reasonable assurance that all risks critical to the success of the organization are identified?

- ❑ Is there a reasonable level of assurance that the level of risk is accurately stated (i.e., the potential effect/consequences of uncertainty and the likelihood of that effect occurring)?

- ❑ Is the list of risks current and are new or modified risks identified on a timely basis?

ERM programs are not perfect; they cannot be. Even the best risk management will fail to detect a potential event or situation, or will get the assessment of the effect on objectives and the likelihood of that effect wrong. Such failures do not mean that the ERM program is defective – as reliance is placed on humans and humans are imperfect.

However, ERM programs can be of a quality that they provide an acceptable, reasonable level of assurance that risks will be identified and assessed accurately and on a timely basis.

I said I would talk about the fact that internal audit needs to be concerned with the risks that management needs to address as they manage the organization every day, as well as those that we can anticipate them facing in the next 12-18 months.

In assessing the adequacy of an ERM program, and whether it can be relied on by internal audit, internal audit must satisfy itself that the ERM program will identify new or changes to existing risks promptly. It can't expect perfect, only reasonable assurance.

Any list of risks has to include the risks that matter today and will matter over the next period. Otherwise, internal audit is providing assurance on what used to be the risks, not the risks that matter now to the board and top management.

As I noted earlier, there will be times where a critical risk to the organization will not be the focus of an internal audit engagement. Where there is no *value* in such an engagement, where it would not provide additional insight that management would gladly pay for[16], it should not be performed.

At Solectron, it was clear that the company had excess manufacturing capacity and needed to rationalize its footprint by closing some sites and consolidating operations where possible. A task force was established to perform the necessary analysis and recommend the path forward.

While I provided moral support, there was little value in any other internal audit activity.

At Business Objects, we identified competitor risk as perhaps the most significant. But there was little value in an audit engagement as the subject was not only assigned to senior members of the management team but was regularly discussed at executive committee and board meetings.

Where management does *not* have a reliable ERM program (which is, unfortunately the case in most organizations), internal audit needs to perform its own risk assessment. But, it also needs to ensure management and the board know that an ineffective ERM program is itself a huge risk to the organization. It's like driving on the freeway without looking up and around continuously.

---

[16] Quoting Dwight Wiggins, formerly EVP at Tosco, who told me once that IA had not performed an audit he would not gladly have paid for. I think that's a brilliant test.

The Risk Universe

People tend to forget that risk is the effect of uncertainty on *objectives*[17]. They tend to list risks in terms of their assessed level (frequently evaluated based on a financial value) without reference to any objective.

But, the point of risk management is to enable management to make better, more informed decisions, and thus to enable the achievement of objectives and the success of the organization.

While I prefer the ISO 31000:2009 risk management standard, the 2004 COSO ERM Framework has some excellent language that is worth repeating.

Enterprise risk management deals with risks and opportunities affecting value creation or preservation, defined as follows:

*Enterprise risk management is a process, effected by an entity's board of directors, management and other personnel, applied in strategy setting and across the enterprise, designed to identify potential events[18] that may affect the entity, and manage risk to be within its risk appetite, to provide reasonable assurance regarding the achievement of entity objectives.*

The definition reflects certain fundamental concepts. Enterprise risk management is:

- A process, ongoing and flowing through an entity

- Effected by people at every level of an organization

- Applied in strategy setting

- Applied across the enterprise, at every level and unit, and includes taking an entity-level portfolio view of risk

- Designed to identify potential events that, if they occur, will affect the entity and to manage risk within its risk appetite

---

[17] Definition in the global risk management standard, ISO 31000:2009.

[18] It would have been better if COSO had talked about events and situations.

- Able to provide reasonable assurance to an entity's management and board of directors
- Geared to achievement of objectives in one or more separate but overlapping categories

COSO provides an explanation for the reference to risks and opportunities:

> Events can have negative impact, positive impact, or both. Events with a negative impact represent risks, which can prevent value creation or erode existing value. Events with positive impact may offset negative impacts or represent opportunities. Opportunities are the possibility that an event will occur and positively affect the achievement of objectives, supporting value creation or preservation. Management channels opportunities back to its strategy or objective-setting processes, formulating plans to seize the opportunities.

Internal audit should *not* focus exclusively on the controls relied upon to manage the negative effects of uncertainty (what COSO calls 'risks').

It should also consider whether controls are in place to provide reasonable assurance that opportunities will be seized. As COSO says, "Enterprise risk management enables management to effectively deal with uncertainty and associated risk and opportunity, enhancing the capacity to build value".

Where I am going is this: internal audit (and the same applies to risk management practitioners) should take each of the organization's objectives and answer three questions:

1. What could go *wrong* and adversely affect the achievement of the objective?

2. What needs to go *right* if the objective is to be achieved? What *assumptions* have been made?

3. What else could happen that would enable the objective to be exceeded? After all, management is not limited to achieving objectives; surpassing them is more than acceptable!

The traditional internal audit risk assessment process does not start with a list of organizational objectives. The traditional internal audit department starts with an 'audit universe', which is a list of the organization's business processes, business units, and locations that could be the subject of an audit engagement. It prioritizes them using a combination of factors, such as revenue, complexity, the time since the last audit of the area, the severity of prior audit findings, whether there have been changes in systems or personnel, and so on. The more significant units and processes are then included in the audit plan. A second risk assessment identifies, for each targeted entity, which risks are most important at that unit or for that process.

However, this approach only identifies the risks that are significant to the selected unit or business process. It does not identify the risks that matter to the *organization as a whole*.

Issues at a single location can be a source of significant risk to the entire organization. That was the case at Solectron for a while; we had a period of low profits and a problem at any one of our larger factories could have been material to the company as a whole.

But, very often a risk that is important to a single location or business unit may not be important in terms of the entire organization. Internal audit should focus its attention first on the risks that are significant to the entire organization before considering localized risks.

Until now, the profession has talked about risk-based internal auditing. I believe it is time to change the discussion: let's instead practice *enterprise* risk based internal auditing.

It is critical to shift from using an audit universe to using an enterprise *risk universe*.

This is a list of risks to the organization *as a whole*, rather than a list of risks to a unit or process within the organization. The risk universe is prioritized and engagements included in the audit plan as appropriate.

We are not in the business of auditing locations or business processes. Yes, we perform engagements targeting activities and controls in locations and business processes. But, that is only so we can audit (and provide assurance over) the controls relied upon to manage business risks. I prefer to talk about auditing controls over risks through engagements that are performed at locations, etc.

In the absence of an ERM program that can be relied upon, and even when one exists and I want to augment it with my own assessment, I have used a number of techniques. These are probably all familiar to experienced internal auditors:

- ❑ *Listening* to management, the board, and everybody else
- ❑ Auditing by walking around
- ❑ Being present
- ❑ *Paying attention* to operating reports
- ❑ Risk analytics
- ❑ Understanding what is on the *agendas* of the board and executives
- ❑ Brainstorming and workshops

## Listening

The most common risk assessment technique is usually referred to as *talking* to management, the board, and so on. But, I tell all my people that they should focus on *listening* rather than talking. In fact, if they are talking more than 40% of the time, they are not listening enough!

There is so much to learn, if we are able to open ourselves up and give ourselves the opportunity to listen – to anybody, in any position.

### Enterprise Objectives

A problem for many internal auditors is that they don't know what the objectives of their organization are! They might be aware of what is shared with the public, but it is important for the CAE to learn what the board has set as targets for the top executives, such as the revenue and earnings goals for the period, as well as any other objectives such as market share, customer acceptance, new product development, and so on.

It is also useful to know how the corporate objectives cascade down to senior and lower levels of management. Many organizations don't do this very well, leading to a failure to align the interests of middle management with those of top management and of the organization as a whole. However, while the latter is valuable information for the internal auditor, the audit plan should focus on the risks to the enterprise rather than individual or business unit objectives.

Some objectives are never formally stated. For example, it would be unusual (to say the least) for any annual plan to set an objective of "comply with the law" or "keep employees safe". Even though they may be 'understood' or 'assumed' rather than formally stated, risks to these objectives should be considered in developing the audit plan.

The CAE should never assume that he or she knows what the enterprise objectives are. If there is a formal plan, then I advise the CAE to meet with the CEO and the CFO, as well as with the chair of the audit committee and other members of the board if possible, to ask questions and listen carefully as the leaders of the organization describe and explain their view and understanding of the enterprise objectives.

Ask a question and listen.

Ask a confirming question and listen again. If something seems to be unsaid, ask and listen again.

Often, it is insufficient to simply read a plan or other documentation of enterprise objectives. Questions are needed, with careful attention to the answers, to obtain the necessary level of understanding of the objectives – and which carry the higher priority.

Attention to how executive compensation will be awarded can be useful in understanding which objectives will carry more weight and influence management decisions and actions.

I have found the following situations useful for listening:

- ❑ One-on-one discussions (listening opportunities) with the CEO and, separately, with other top executives such as the CFO,

Corporate Controller, COO, CMO, division presidents, and CIO. It is amazing how different their interpretations can be!

❑ Earnings and other calls or meetings with investors. This is an opportunity to hear what investors and analysts believe is important, and these metrics often drive executive actions.

❑ One-on-one discussions with the chair of the audit committee, compensation committee, and other board members. I find these much more useful than a group discussion.

❑ All hands/all employee meetings and off-site strategy meetings of the management team

It is key to ensure these situations are true *listening* opportunities. The idea is not to talk about internal audit; it is to make sure that you understand the goals and objectives of the organization – what is important for the period ahead.

How will the board and top management measure success?

Tim Leech of *Risk Oversight* often talks about 'objective-based auditing'. The idea behind this is that risk-based auditing doesn't go far enough, as what we are concerned with is the achievement of organizational objectives. We should focus directly on objectives rather than on risks. While I have some sympathy for his perspective, I prefer to talk about [enterprise] risk-based auditing – as long as we all understand that we are concerned about risks to enterprise *objectives*[19].

---

[19] There is also a school of thought that goes even further than objective-based auditing. In an April 2010 article in *Internal Auditor*, Kevin Shen proposes 'Shareholder value-based auditing'. The concept is that internal audit starts by understanding the sources of value created by the enterprise for its stakeholders. Then internal audit can assess the management of risks, not to objectives, but to stakeholder value. I would be more appreciative of this approach if after understanding stakeholder value internal audit would assess the objective and strategy-setting processes before moving on to risks to those objectives. Considering risk to value does not take into account that the organization is moving, executing strategies to enhance it.

*Risks to Objectives*

Once the objectives, both stated and unstated, are understood[20] we need to know which are the more significant risks to their achievement. Again, listening is one of the most important techniques.

I like to sit down with the senior executives responsible for each objective and listen to them explain their view of how is will be achieved and the related risks. It is surprising how many of them don't do this themselves in a structured or disciplined fashion. What I mean by that is the executive thinking about an objective and asking:

- ❏ What could go *wrong*?
- ❏ What needs to go *right*? What *assumptions* have been made?
- ❏ What *opportunities* might arise that would enhance success?

Let me expand on this.

Auditors and risk practitioners are used to thinking about what could go wrong and asking management that question. Another form of that question is "what keeps you up at night?" But, it may be better to ask "what needs to go right for you to succeed?"

This turns the conversation from one that might be perceived as about compliance or bureaucracy to one about success.

Such a conversation implies a common goal – the success of the organization – and the executive is more likely to identify both the events and situations that could negatively impact success and those that could enhance it.

One way to learn more is to ask about assumptions.

Every forecast or projection, every budget and plan, includes assumptions. None of these is certain and there is always a possibility that they will not come about. Each assumption has at least one source of risk behind it.

---

[20] One risk that merits consideration is the possibility that sub-optimal objectives are set by management and the board. I consider this to be a governance-related risk, which topic is covered later.

When I was with Tosco, I liked to meet with the senior executives in charge of each of the two divisions for as long as an hour, once each month. Dwight Wiggins was the President of the Tosco Refining Company and an executive vice president of the corporation. At the end of one of our discussions, I thanked him for taking the time out of his very busy schedule to meet with me. He turned to me and said, "No, Norman. I should thank you! Our meetings are the only times I get to sit and think about the business". He spent the great majority of his time fighting fires, working on specific problems and plans, and briefing top management.

When I met with Dwight, I asked open-ended questions about the business and its challenges. We then engaged in a conversation about those challenges and where he spent his time monitoring activity. What I was listening to were his perceptions of the risks to the success of his part of the organization. Sometimes, but not always, I would ask questions about 'risk'; but I can generally understand what the risks are without using the word 'risk'. I try to use the language of the business, rather than the language of the risk and control practitioner.

However, every so often I would develop a list of risks based in part on our discussions – and I will review that list and my assessment (again, based on what I have heard) of the level of risk with him.

Many executives and board members like to see something to frame the discussion. Over the years, I found that a simple list is not very effective. Instead, I used mind maps and other techniques.

The diagram below is what I used at Maxtor; I first created this at Tosco, modifying it for each subsequent company.

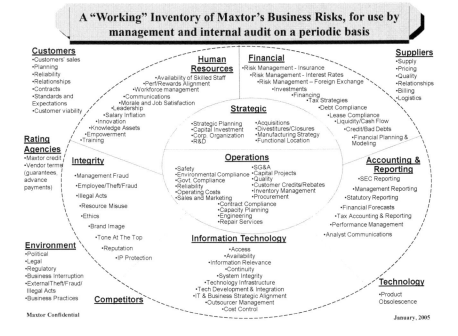

Maxtor Confidential

A "Working" Inventory of Maxtor's Business Risks, for use by management and internal audit on a periodic basis

**Customers**
•Customers' sales
•Planning
•Reliability
•Relationships
•Contracts
•Standards and Expectations
•Customer viability

**Human Resources**
•Availability of Skilled Staff
•Perf/Rewards Alignment
•Workforce management
•Communications
•Morale and Job Satisfaction
•Leadership
•Salary Inflation
•Innovation
•Knowledge Assets
•Empowerment
•Training

**Financial**
•Risk Management - Insurance
•Risk Management - Interest Rates
•Risk Management – Foreign Exchange
•Investments
•Financing
•Tax Strategies
•Debt Compliance
•Lease Compliance
•Liquidity/Cash Flow
•Credit/Bad Debts
•Financial Planning & Modeling

**Suppliers**
•Supply
•Pricing
•Quality
•Relationships
•Billing
•Logistics

**Strategic**
•Strategic Planning
•Capital Investment
•Corp. Organization
•R&D
•Acquisitions
•Divestitures/Closures
•Manufacturing Strategy
•Functional Location

**Rating Agencies**
•Maxtor credit
•Vendor terms (guarantees, advance payments)

**Integrity**
•Management Fraud
•Employee/Theft/Fraud
•Illegal Acts
•Resource Misuse
•Ethics
•Brand Image
•Tone At The Top
•Reputation
•IP Protection

**Operations**
•Safety
•Environmental Compliance
•Govt. Compliance
•Reliability
•Operating Costs
•Sales and Marketing
•SG&A
•Capital Projects
•Quality
•Customer Credits/Rebates
•Inventory Management
•Procurement
•Contract Compliance
•Capacity Planning
•Engineering
•Repair Services

**Accounting & Reporting**
•SEC Reporting
•Management Reporting
•Statutory Reporting
•Financial Forecasts
•Tax Accounting & Reporting
•Performance Management
•Analyst Communications

**Environment**
•Political
•Legal
•Regulatory
•Business Interruption
•External Theft/Fraud/ Illegal Acts
•Business Practices

**Competitors**

**Information Technology**
•Access
•Availability
•Information Relevance
•Continuity
•System Integrity
•Technology Infrastructure
•Tech Development & Integration
•IT & Business Strategic Alignment
•Outsourcer Management
•Cost Control

**Technology**
•Product Obsolescence

January, 2005

I have used this graphic a number of different ways. Initially, I sought to make it as complete as possible and then get the executives to (a) think about it, then (b) provide their assessment of the level of risk and the related objectives. Once I had the input from each of the top executives, I reviewed it with the CEO.

I remember that when I reviewed a consolidated version with Jon Schwartz, CEO of Business Objects, he disagreed with his executives' assessments. What was interesting to me was that he was surprised that his direct reports did not see risk to objectives the same way he did. This sparked a useful executive committee meeting.

I also used the graphic to stimulate discussion about whether management had an acceptable process, including assigned responsibilities, for managing risk. When I used the chart with members of the audit committee, they found it so useful that they asked me to lead a start-up ERM function!

Another use for the chart was in risk workshops and brainstorming sessions – discussed later.

I don't listen only to executives. I try to listen to everybody.

Tom Peters, the author of many books about management, has said that if you want to know what is really happening within an organization, you should "ask the janitor". I am not going to say that I will ask the janitor per se, but I do go out of my way to listen to the people in the front line: the people who work with customers, manufacture products, and so on.

Executives may have the big picture, but to fill in the detail – and get a real world perspective – it is necessary to talk to the people directly in the line of fire.


### Auditing by Walking Around

Talking about listening to everybody, especially those in the line of fire, I believe in something I refer to as "auditing by walking around". Modeled on the earlier concept of "*managing* by walking around", the idea is that auditors need to learn the business, its risks, and how it works by getting out among the front-line workers and their management.

Tosco had several thousand convenience stores (primarily branded 'Circle K') and gas stations (most of which were branded '76').

I could (and did) talk to management about the business; I also frequented the stores myself, talking to the staff there and listening to the challenges they described to me – both with their customers and their management. But, I most enjoyed riding along with a district manager on his routine visits to his stores.

This was an opportunity to have an extended one-on-one conversation with an individual who knew directly what it was like to run the business. He knew the daily challenges, how customers and employees thought and acted[21], and what it took to be successful.

The convenience store business is a low margin one, with a great deal of competition. We needed to take advantage of all opportunities when they presented themselves.

---

[21] I gained insight into the 'culture' of the organization this way.

As I mentioned earlier, internal auditors need to be concerned not only with controls to prevent or mitigate adverse events and situations, but controls to identify and take advantage of opportunities.

When we arrived at one location in Phoenix, Arizona, which had both a store and a gas station, the district manager and store manager told me about one of their frustrations.

The station was at a busy intersection with traffic lights. Each of the roads carried heavy rush-hour traffic and ours was one of three gas stations at the intersection.

We had received a notice from the city that repairs to the road were scheduled. The roadworks would tear up much of the intersection, blocking access to all three gas stations.

The store manager had a great idea that the district manager immediately approved: build a new access from the road just around the corner. This would require a very modest investment, but would probably capture most of the traffic through the intersection – not only our normal traffic, but that of at least one of the other stations.

A capital request (Authorization for Expenditure or AFE) was submitted. But, it took 'corporate' three months to approve, by which time the roadworks had been completed and the opportunity lost.

I heard similar stories from other parts of the retail organization. For example, an AFE to build canopies over the gas pumps was not approved until *after* the rainy season.

Learning about these risks to revenue and profits, basically a failure of the corporate AFE process, led to a very interesting audit engagement.

Our audit of the AFE process helped management see that they had built in too much bureaucracy in this and other processes – a failure to trust and delegate authority by the division president[22].

Internal auditors frequently miss a great opportunity to learn by listening, literally when walking around.

---

[22] The story of this audit engagement is told in Chapter 29 of *World-Class Internal Auditing: Tales from my Journey*

It is standard practice to get a tour of a factory at the start of an audit. This is a wonderful opportunity not only to understand the business, but to engage the workers, supervisors, and their managers and hear what they have to say about the business, their frustrations, what may go wrong, and what needs to go right. It's when you can be open to hearing about problems with the culture of safety, the quality of vendor products and services, training, and more.

Dwight Wiggins once asked that my team and I take the accounting staff with us when we went around the refineries. This was not for our education, but because he didn't think the accountants understood the business and how it was run in practice. Dwight is a very smart man.

Talking of smart people, Soo Wai Mun of my Singapore team at Solectron took the opportunity to build strong relationships with management when she visited a factory. She didn't just listen to their gripes about the corporate office, but took those complaints to the people in corporate (with whom she also had strong relationships) and helped both sides work together to resolve them.

Other *auditing by walking around* opportunities can include:

❑  Having lunch or going to coffee with employees and managers (i.e., socializing with people outside the audit department)

❑  Listening to the external auditors, regulators, and consultants. I made it a point to stop by their cubicles as I started and finished my day, just to ask how they were doing and what they might be concerned about

❑  Attending staff meetings. More on this in a moment

❑  Being open for people to stop by and chat – about anything that is on their mind, even if totally unrelated (on the surface) to planned audits

### Being Present

Before you can listen, you need to be present. You need to be where people are talking and working.

Some internal audit departments live in an ivory tower, part of a corporate organization that is at the center of the enterprise. While there are advantages in being at the center, with information flowing in and with access to corporate officers and executives, the disadvantage is that you may not know what is *really* happening in the business – where the front lines extend across the globe and the men and women in the trenches feel disconnected with the corporate bureaucracy.

I like to have my office in the headquarters area, but I put my staff where the action is. When business units are headquartered in other areas of the country or the globe, those are where I position my direct reports.

For example, at Tosco we had multiple refineries. Each was a major operation in itself, so I had staff located there. But, my director for the Tosco Refining Company was based at that division's headquarters in New Jersey and the director for the Marketing Company was at their HQ in Tempe, Arizona. At Business Objects, we had a regional structure; I was at the California office, co-located with the CEO and CFO. But I also had staff in the Vancouver, Paris and Singapore offices, co-located with the Americas, Europe, and Asia/Pacific executives.

I require my direct reports to build a strong relationship with the management of the areas they are responsible for. They attend those executives' staff meetings and have periodic one-on-one meetings with them. They are part of the local management team in some ways[23], dedicated to helping that part of the business succeed, although they retain their organizational independence and objectivity.

When they are present, when they are seen, they are able to listen.

My experience is that people will think of coming to you, whether to provide information or to seek advice, if they see you. If they don't see you, the likelihood they will call on you is significantly diminished.

At Solectron, my team was scattered across the organization – again, to remain in touch with the pulse of the organization.

---

[23] For example, at Tosco they were included in emergency response teams. My environmental auditing expert (Valerie Uyeda) was on the team that responded to an incident at the Los Angeles refinery.

One of my team, Jeff Mullis, was based in Charlotte, North Carolina. On one of my visits to Charlotte, I arrived outside Jeff's office a few minutes early for a scheduled meeting with him. As I neared his office, I heard voices inside. I waited outside while he finished the meeting he was having with two members of local management; it was clear that they had come to him for advice on an operational issue (he had been in local operating management prior to joining the audit team).

When they left and I entered his office, Jeff apologized for keeping me waiting. He asked if I had a problem that he spent time talking to local management like this rather than spending all his time on assigned audit engagements. My reply was to congratulate him!

I was very pleased that he had retained his connections with operating management and made himself available when they needed his advice and insight (that 'magic' word, again). He knew what was going on in the business, had his finger on the pulse, and as a result could not only be a more effective auditor but help the entire internal audit team understand the risks and opportunities across the organization.

Before closing this section, I want to touch on the important topic of language and culture.

When you operate internal audit with a team based only in corporate, not only are they disconnected from the staff in the other business locations (like all members of 'corporate', they are very often seen as outsiders – with every item of baggage that brings in terms of trust and so on). They may also use a different language and are used to a different culture.

I could anticipate this when talking about international operations. For example, I needed my Singapore team to be able to speak Mandarin and Malay and understand the cultures for them to be effective auditing our operations in China and Malaysia. But, the same principle holds true for different parts of the USA and UK!

My Tosco team included managers based in New Jersey, Philadelphia, and New Orleans. They connected far more easily with local management than other members of the audit team.

Internal auditors need to be able to listen to everything that is being said. That will be very difficult if they don't fully understand the language, the idioms used, and the body language of the speaker.

## Paying attention to operating reports

The enterprise runs on information. It flows around, up to management, and down into the trenches.

Internal audit needs to feed at the trough of information. There is no reason that internal audit should not receive and use the information management uses to make decisions and run the business.

I first discovered the power of operating reports as a junior auditor with Cooper Brothers[24] in London. I was a member of the team that audited the UK subsidiary of Hercules Powder Company, with Kevin Gilbert as the lead auditor. Kevin developed a set of analytics, using the company's operating reports, where we could see trends in revenues, costs, margins, and inventory levels by product. (Today, these analytics would be generated by software, but back then it was all manual.) The analytics allowed us to see variations that could indicate revenue and cost (and therefore inventory valuation) issues, potential accounting errors, and more.

The analytics taught me that variations disclosed by operating reports are a great source of information about new or changing risks.

I adopted the practice, when I became CAE, of similarly analyzing operating reports. I attended the CFO's monthly meetings with the finance and management team where he asked questions about the reasons for trends and variances from forecast. Again, this was a wonderful opportunity to listen as risks and opportunities were identified and management decided on actions to address them.

Some might focus on revenues and profits. I look for fluctuations by product in cost, inventory levels, and more. They collectively tell me a lot

---

[24] Cooper Brothers later merged with Lybrand, Ross Bros., and Montgomery to form Coopers & Lybrand, then with Price Waterhouse to form PricewaterhouseCoopers, or PwC.

about what is happening now with the business, and shed some light into what might be around the corner.

Risk monitoring does not mean separate reports designed to identify new or changed risks. The best source of information is the set of reports that management uses to run the business. If necessary, internal audit can audit the controls over those reports to ensure their completeness and accuracy.

I have consistently asked my team to get to know the financial and operations analysts. These are the people who dive deep into the operating results to discern and understand the reasons for trends and variations. There is no reason why internal audit should not leverage their work; on occasion, I have asked for copies of their spreadsheets and adapted them for my own risk monitoring purposes.

The CFO and the Finance team are not the only people using operating information, analyzing it for trends and basing actions on it. Business unit leads, especially the unit controllers, do so also. I encourage my team not only to receive their reports, but to talk (and, especially, listen) to them, and attend the meetings where the results are dissected.

These days, the management of many if not most organizations run the business based on key metrics, dashboards, and so on. Internal audit should receive the same information and use it to understand the business, its performance and risks, and ensure the audit plan is in sync.

If internal auditors do not have the same dashboards and metrics every month, you should be asking "why ever not?"

### Risk Analytics

In addition to using management reports, internal audit always has the option of developing its own risk analytics.

I strongly advise CAEs to use management reports first and only develop their own analytics where management's reporting is insufficient. In that case, the CAE should try to understand why management doesn't already have the appropriate reporting in place: it may well reflect a weakness of significance.

I prefer to get management to develop and use the reports rather than internal audit taking on what should be a management activity.

However, there may be situations where internal audit risk analytics are justified. One common area is fraud risk, where the audit committee often (but not always) expects internal audit to perform a level of independent fraud risk monitoring and fraud detection.

The temptation is to develop analytics that are designed to detect potential anomalies and errors (deliberate or inadvertent) in the data.

While I would argue that management should perform such a detective control, the greater error (in my opinion) is to dive into analytics development without first understanding the risk that is being monitored.

Audit departments end up with reports on risks that, frankly, don't matter – and will never matter – to the success of the organization.

For example, many organizations create an analytics capability within internal audit whose first deployment of the technology is against accounts payable. While duplicate payments and maybe even potential fraud may be detected, the level of potential harm is usually low – in other words, these are not risks that matter.

It is better to design analytics that target specific risks.

That is what we did at Tosco and other companies. We used analytics very selectively, targeting revenue fraud risk, inventory fraud risk, and so on.

## What is on the *agendas* of the board and executives

What matters to the board and top management?

Typically, the issues of concern are the items they discuss at board meetings, executive committee meetings, strategy and other off-site meetings, and so on.

CAEs, although we like to think of them as senior executives, rarely attend the full board meeting or executive committee meeting. It is more common for the CAE to attend just the audit committee meeting and the staff meetings of the CFO[25].

Even if the CAE does not attend the meetings of the full board or executive team, he or she should be able to see the agendas and minutes.

In my experience, there is often some resistance from the board secretary (often the organization's general counsel), but once an explanation is provided that resistance is usually overcome.

It is a mistake, in my opinion, for the CAE to stand on his or her rights and simply say "I need it and am entitled to full access". It is a mistake to pull out the audit charter as if it was handed down as the word of God. It is better to explain that the information is necessary for internal audit to ensure its activities are aligned with those of the board and top management, and its audit engagements are focused on issues that matter to the leaders of the organization.

One-on-one meetings are opportunities to add some flesh to the bare bones of the agenda and minutes. The CAE should have regular meetings with the chair and other members of the audit committee, with the CEO and CFO, and with others who attend the meetings, such as the general counsel.

The CAE should consider the items on the agenda:

- ❑ If there are issues on the board or executive agendas that are not included in the risk universe, why is that?

- ❑ If the audit plan includes risks that are not on their agendas, why is that?

---

[25] If the CAE reports administratively to another senior executive, he or she would attend their staff meetings.

Brainstorming and Workshops

We all have a brain. Unfortunately, we don't always make maximum use of all the brains available to us.

At Tosco, I was proud of my knowledge of the business, relationships with the board and executives, and understanding of the more significant risks. But, I learned my lesson when I held brainstorming sessions with each of my audit teams. In the past, I had held such sessions with my direct reports, but that proved to be less effective than I had thought.

I had separate audit teams for the Refining and Marketing companies – necessary not only because they were in different locations, but because there were significant differences in the businesses.

I remember a breakthrough meeting with the Tosco Marketing audit team in Phoenix, Arizona. I started by listing the organization's objectives as I knew them. The team didn't have anything to add.

But, when we started to talk about the risks to those objectives, everybody contributed actively.

A number of important sources of risk were raised, many of which were new to me (some I was aware of but didn't understand how significant they were and the problems they were causing to the business. In fact, I suspect that while middle management was working on them actively, senior management was less informed – and by that I mean they were less informed than they should have been).

The value of listening to everybody, not just senior management, was brought home to me. While I was listening to top executives, my team was listening to those who reported to those executives.

Risk workshops are well-known as a technique for identifying and assessing risks.

The first risk workshop I held was before anybody was talking about risk or workshops. It was when I was a vice president of internal audit at Home Savings and I was concerned about access to our banking systems.

Management had told me that the risk was low because of limitations enforced by the system. I gathered together a diverse group of IT and business user managers and staff. I asked questions and then listened to the conversation that ensued. As we now understand, bringing these groups together triggered thoughts and insights that they would not have had if I had talked to them separately. We were able to identify a number of weaknesses or vulnerabilities that could have been exploited, some by third parties and some by employees.

At Tosco, one group wanted to set up a new channel for selling our products on the south side of the border with Mexico. There would be huge tax advantages to doing so[26], but another group voiced concerns. They could not explain those concerns; they had no specific issues, just a sense of disquiet.

I had one of my managers, Roger Herd, lead a risk workshop and the group discussed the situation openly and without anybody being defensive about their position. The collaborative effort identified specific issues and the group unanimously agreed not to go ahead with the initiative.

At Business Objects, I made a presentation to the CEO and his direct reports that reflected what appeared to be a consensus view of the more significant risks to the enterprise objects. I consider the discussion that followed, which the CEO (Jon Schwartz) allowed to flow freely without influence from him, to be a form of risk workshop.

The key for me is to recognize that a risk workshop is a technique that can be applied in many ways, with various groups. The smart CAE finds the best way to use it in his or her organization.

## Commentary

In fact, the smart CAE knows that there are many ways to identify the risks that matter.

He or she selects the combination that will work best for the organization at that time – knowing that different methods may work better at other times.

---

[26] This was before the NAFTA agreement that created a free trade zone between the USA and Mexico.

The smart CAE also knows that *management* should be the one identifying and assessing risks. When that does not happen, the first reaction should be to help them step up rather than doing it for them. After all, how can the CAE expect management to design and operate effective controls over the more significant risks if they don't know what they are!

In addition, the people in the trenches and running the organization should have a better understanding of the business and risks to its objectives than any auditors or risk practitioners. If they don't that's another issue the CAE should be raising with top management and the board.

But, there will be times when internal audit needs to obtain its own understanding of the risks that matter. In those situations, the CAE should use all the brains he or she can, and the most suitable combination of techniques, to build and maintain a current and useful risk universe.

## Chapter 4: IT risk and audit

Jay Taylor[27] has said on several occasions, "There is no such thing as 'IT risk'".

He is 100% correct.

The risk is the effect of a failure in an IT process or activity on a *business* objective.

- It's not a loss of availability; it's the inability to bill customers and record revenue.

- It's not a failure to secure intellectual property (IP); it's the loss of future revenue.

- It's not privacy; it's customer reputation damage and the effect on revenue plus any losses from lawsuits, etc.

Failures in IT processes or activities may certainly represent a *source of risk* to the business and its achievement of objectives.

They may very well be sources of risk that matter.

But, it is essential to consider the effect of such a failure on business objectives in assessing the level of risk – and whether and how much it should matter.

### Technology risk assessment

Internal audit should not assess IT-related risks separately from other business risks. We need to focus on the achievement of entity objectives, not on a notion that there are specific IT risks that matter all by themselves.

There should be a single risk assessment process and a single audit plan.

---

[27] At that time, Jay led the IT audit team at General Motors.

It is totally fine to have technology audit specialists focus on technology-related risks – as long as they do so within the context of how those sources of risk might affect entity business objectives.

Not to pick on anybody in particular, because this is one example out of many, but in 2011 a senior manager with Deloitte shared this list of top IT risks[28]:

1. Social networking
2. Mobile devices
3. Malware
4. End user computing
5. Corporate espionage
6. Project backlog
7. IT Governance
8. Electronic records management
9. Data management
10. Cloud computing

I can see how failures in managing these areas may be sources of risk to corporate business objectives.

But in order to know what matters, we need to understand and assess how significant any of the above would be in terms of their effect on one or more of those objectives.

For example, do I care equally about the backlog of IT projects for *all* areas of the business? Are extensive backlogs in IT projects relating to the management of facilities expense as significant as those relating to the integration of an acquired business?

Where the backlog is high and relates to an important business system, is that an acceptable level of risk? Should the organization move funds from key business initiatives to IT?

---

[28] *Information Technology Risks in Today's Environment*, Traci Mizoguchi, 2012

We also need to move from talking about 'IT' risks to talking about technology-related risks.

Technology is no longer (if it ever was) the sole responsibility of the IT department. In fact, some[29] report that the Marketing function in many organizations is spending as much or more on technology than the IT department.

When technology can be acquired quickly and easily without capital expenditure (as in the case of cloud solutions), we need to understand how dependent the business is and the potential for any technology failure to affect the business.

Deloitte is correct to identify 'cloud' as a source of risk. But, should I worry equally about cloud applications supporting travel and expense reporting and about those that support management of the sales pipeline?

My list of technology-related risks might identify a specific source of risk, such as information security, but with a defined focus. The focus would be where a potential failure would have a significant adverse effect on a corporate objective.

I might be concerned with these technology-related risks:

- Change management for the manufacturing and finance applications

- The integrity of mobile applications and data used by the executive team in decision-making

- The security of spreadsheets used by financial analysts in account reconciliations and similar, both for management and external financial reporting

- Access to IP by former employees, contractors, and temporary staff

---

[29] Gartner, in particular.

One of the side benefits of the SOX compliance work we did was the understanding that we need to understand the level of reliance on specific 'critical IT functionality'. By that I mean the automated controls, the automated portion of semi-automated controls, and the reports used in controls we rely upon to manage risks to objectives.

I was a member of the team (and the author) that developed the GAIT methodology series (mentioned in Chapter 6). Available from the IIA as a free download (they are 'recommended' supplemental guidance) are:

- The *GAIT Methodology*, which helps organizations continue the top-down and risk-based approach to identify IT general controls (ITGC) risks for SOX, and then the key controls relied upon to address those risks

- *GAIT for Business and IT Risk*[30], which follows the same approach as the original GAIT Methodology but for all risks, not just financial reporting risks

- *GAIT for IT General Control Deficiency Assessment*

The GAIT methodology starts by identifying the controls relied upon to manage the business risk of concern. It then identifies the critical IT functionality in those controls; the application(s) that house the functionality; and, the risk to the reliable operation of that critical functionality should there be a failure in an ITGC process. Control objectives and controls are then identified to address the ITGC risk.

When we plan the work required to audit the management of a risk that matters, we need to consider how we will obtain reasonable assurance that the critical functionality in related key controls consistently operate as desired.

Internal audit should consider whether there is a need to:

- Test the operation of specific critical IT functionality such as the production of a report or operation of an automated control

- Assess and test related ITGC

---

[30] Often referred to as 'GAIT-R'

As mentioned in Chapter 6, one option is to include the testing of ITGC controls, reports, or automated controls in the same engagement as testing the business controls. They may also be addressed in one or more separate audits.

But, the key is to focus all the time on the *business risk*.

A failure in the management of a technology can have an effect on multiple business objectives. The aggregate effect on business objectives may drive an audit of this source of business risk to the top of the risk assessment.

However, there are many trendy technology risk areas that, when internal audit leadership reflects on how significant a failure would be compared to other risks, simply don't merit internal audit attention.

While a failure might be momentarily embarrassing, would there be a need for discussion and action from leadership of the organization? If not, is this a risk that matters?

### Technology risks that merit consideration

As mentioned earlier, a good question to ask is "what could go wrong?"

When it comes to technology, there is more opportunity for things to go wrong today than five years ago, or even last year – and probably more opportunity tomorrow and next year than there is today.

While the top-down approach (as exemplified by the GAIT methodology) is critical, it is also important to identify sources of risk to corporate objectives from the bottom-up.

Internal audit needs to obtain and then maintain an understanding of how technology is used at their organization.

Only then can it ask how a failure in the use or management of that technology might affect the achievement of business objectives – taking into account controls within business processes.

As CAE, I took care to build a relationship with the CIO and my IT audit team was similarly diligent about their relationships with technology management and staff across the organization.

As the use of technology and our dependence on it continue to grow, we need to broaden our work to understand the use of technology beyond IT, for example to the Marketing, Manufacturing, Engineering, Sales, Finance, and other functions.

We need to do more than show interest when we see new technology in the news. We need to understand how it might be in use today or tomorrow in our organizations.

New technology that merits watching and consideration (as of mid-2016) includes:

- The Internet of Things. How many enterprise devices (such as equipment used in manufacturing) are connected? How many are connected to third parties (e.g., for monitoring or maintenance)? How many customer devices are connected to enterprise systems?

- Mobile devices, including wearables. As these devices are used to disseminate information for the management of the organization, they are not only a source of advantage but are targets for hackers. In addition, not only data but applications themselves are increasingly run from mobile devices. Errors in mobile analytics, for example, can lead to poor decisions by executives. Failures in software used by the information security team to monitor intrusions can mean they don't learn about attacks and response is delayed.

- The extended networked enterprise. Attacks may succeed by targeting not only the corporate network, or employees' personal systems and devices, but those of vendors, customers, channel partners, service providers and more. Once an intruder has gained access to a trusted third party, they may be able to obtain undetected access the company's systems.

- ...and so many more.

New technology can disrupt any business. Internal audit needs to be concerned not only with the risk from technology adoption, but from the failure to adopt new technology and employ for full advantage.

History is full of example of companies that were overtaken by technology, such as Kodak and RIM (manufacturer of the Blackberry phone).

Internal audit should be concerned with the possibility that their company fails to take full advantage of new technology and is left behind.

In developing the audit plan, the internal audit team should consider whether there are adequate processes in place to identify, evaluate, and then deploy new technology for advantage.

This can certainly be a risk that matters to any organization.

### Commentary

Every company is now an IT company – because it relies so much on technology. It is essential to manage that technology such that it brings as much as possible of the value but as little as possible of the damage of which it is capable.

The test that every CAE should bring before including a technology-related risk in the audit plan is the same as he or she should bring to any potential audit engagement:

If there was a control failure, would the level of risk rise to the level that would merit the attention of the executive team, if not the board?

Let's audit the risks that matter.

A final word: I spent the majority of my pre-CAE career in IT auditing. I believe I have a better-than-average understanding of technology and risk.

Perhaps because of that, I recognized that at each of my companies technology risk was near the top.

As a result, as many as 25% of my audit staff were IT auditors!

But, my focus was always on risks that matter because of their effect on business objectives. Every engagement was focused. If we audited ITGC, we audited specific ITGC and not the ITGC over every application, server, or part of the network.

One of my mantras has been that the greatest risk can usually be found where there is change.

In this dynamic world in which we live and work, technology is the driver of change – and a source of risk that needs to be managed and audited.

## Chapter 5: The level of risk that matters

It's not as simple as finding the areas with the highest level of risk to corporate objectives.

For example, while I was at SAP[31] management and the board decided to embrace a new technology on which all new applications would be built (with the exception of tablet and phone apps) and to which it would migrate its existing applications.

There were several reasons for this high risk strategy. The new technology, called HANA[32], would allow applications to process transactions several hundred times as fast as existing database technologies. Those existing technologies were predominantly sold by Oracle, SAP's fierce competitor in the business application market.

Management and the board were concerned that unless they made this move, over time their software (especially their ERP solutions) would lose its market leadership position.

In other words, this was a risk that SAP management and board believed they had to take for long-term success.

The adoption of the HANA strategy was clearly SAP's highest area of risk.

But, where would the value be in an audit engagement that focused on the management of the risk?

Management and the board were fully aware of the risk and were monitoring it closely, so an internal audit would only confirm what they already knew.

An audit that assessed whether management had adequate processes and controls for monitoring the risk as it changed might have had some

---

[31] I was not in either internal audit or risk management at the time of this story.

[32] HANA stands for 'high-availability analytic appliance'. It uses high capacity disks to store massive volumes of data in memory, minimizing the time spent 'fetching' data from and writing data back to disk drives.

value, as might an audit of the controls over the related migration projects.

But would those audit engagements have as much value as audits focused on other areas of risk?

In other words, it is not sufficient simply to include audits in the audit plan on the basis of the level of risk alone.

Another consideration is whether management has accepted the level of risk.

In the case of HANA, management was well aware of the risk and had accepted it.

But there are often sources of risk that appear to be moderate at best but are outside (or potentially outside) desired risk levels.

I am referring to situations where there is a 'high' likelihood that risks are outside desired levels. Management believes the level of risk is, say, 100; but, there is a possibility that controls might fail causing the level of risk to rise to 200 when only 100 is acceptable.

The likelihood that controls might fail is sometimes referred to as 'control risk' (although I will present a different use of that expression in a moment). Certainly, the level of control risk is one factor that should be considered.

But there are others.


Inherent, residual, and control risk

'Inherent risk' is generally defined as the level of risk should controls fail. However, some risk practitioners dislike the term, arguing that it is extremely unlikely that all controls will fail[33]. They prefer the term 'maximum potential exposure' – but IMHO the meaning is pretty much the same.

---

[33] For example, the 'inherent risk' from a paper cut is death. This is not reasonable.

'Residual risk' is the level of risk assuming that all the controls are working effectively as desired[34]. Another term for this is 'current risk'. (I generally use the term 'risk', sometimes 'current risk').

Most risk management practitioners measure and report residual risk. They assume that controls are working as desired.

When I have polled internal audit leaders, I have found a variety of methods to define the level of risk.

Most, I believe, use residual risk but some prefer inherent risk. A few use a combination of both.

I like the methodology used by Andrew MacLeod, CAE at Brisbane City Council.

He starts with the level of (current) risk defined in the enterprise risk assessment. But then he considers the likelihood that the controls relied upon to manage risk at that level might fail.

Sources and indicators of control risk might include:

- A history of control failures, especially those detected in prior audits
- Inexperienced process and control owners
- Changes to systems
- Concerns about management and their supervision of the work performed
- Changes to the business, especially if there is high volatility
- ...and so on

Andrew would also consider other factors in his assessment of the likelihood that controls might fail. An example would be the time since the last audit of related controls.

---

[34] Some refer to residual risk as the level of risk after corrective action or risk treatment has been completed. I use the term to denote the current level of risk.

The table below illustrates my interpretation of the Brisbane City Council approach.

| | Inherent Risk | Residual Risk | Effect of Controls | Confidence in Controls | Adjusted Effect of Controls | Adjusted Residual Risk |
|---|---|---|---|---|---|---|
| | a | b | c=a-b | d | e=c*d | f=a-g |
| Customer Credit | 300 | 50 | 250 | 90% | 225 | 75 |
| Inventory Valuation | 200 | 50 | 150 | 80% | 120 | 80 |
| Investments | 150 | 50 | 100 | 70% | 70 | 80 |

The first column shows the level of inherent risk. Customer Credit rates highest of the three in the example, followed by Inventory Valuation and Investments.

The second column shows the level of residual risk, with the third column representing the effect of controls. For example, inherent risk for Customer Credit is assessed as 300, but if the controls over Customer Credit are working as they should the level of risk (i.e., residual risk) is reduced to 50.

Taking multiple factors (such as discussed above) into account, internal audit determines how confident they are that the controls are in fact operating effectively as desired. (This is not as quantitative as it looks. The 90% confidence level for Customer Credit is very much a matter of judgment and experience.)

Based on that, internal audit calculates an adjusted value for controls and, accordingly, for residual risk.

For Customer Credit, the 90% confidence level (or 10% lack of confidence) reduces the effect of controls from 250 to 225. Audit's adjusted residual risk changes from 50 to 75.

Looking at all three areas of risk, this model has changed the risk priority. Customer Credit has moved from first to third.

I like this approach and used something like it as CAE myself. However, I did not have a separate ERM function so while I followed the same principle, I did not have such a structured process.

In fact, I never actually assessed the level of risk as a value. I used my judgment, in consultation with my team, executive management, and the board to identify and then prioritize the areas of high risk where an audit would add value.

## The level of risk

Putting a value on the level of risk is popular, but many (including me) consider it a flawed concept.

The popular way to calculate a level of risk is a simple formula. Multiply the potential effect or consequence of the event or situation by the likelihood of that effect. If the potential effect is a loss of $500 and the likelihood of that loss occurring is 10%, the level of risk is calculated as $50.

But, that formula calculates the level of risk as $50 for each of these situations:

- 100% likelihood of a $50 loss

- 50% likelihood of a $100 loss

- 25% likelihood of a $200 loss

- 10% likelihood of a $500 loss

- 1% likelihood of a $5,000 loss

These situations are not all the same.

The last one or two may be acceptable to management while the others are unacceptable.

Further, there are other factors that need to be considered in determining whether a risk is in an acceptable state. These include

- The volatility of the risk level

- The speed of onset should an adverse event or situation occur

- The duration of the effect

- ...and so on

I am not going to discuss this point in detail, as it is covered in *World-Class Risk Management*.


## Commentary

As I mentioned earlier, I don't try to calculate a value for the level of risk when developing my risk-based audit plan.

Instead, I use my judgment with input from and after consultation with the members of my team, senior management, and the board to develop a risk-prioritized list of audit engagements.

I consider not only the level of risk (however that is assessed), but the potential for a controls failure that would take that risk beyond desired levels.

Most of all, I consider the value of the potential audit. Would it provide the combination of assurance, advice, and insight that my stakeholders in management and on the board need if they are to be effective?

## Chapter 6: Audit engagements that matter

So we have identified the *risks that matter*.

But how do we translate our risk universe into a risk-based audit plan?

Even if we have a prioritized risk universe, should we perform an audit engagement for every risk?

We should recognize that there are going to be times where it is not advisable to perform an (assurance) audit even if the risk is high. These are times where the value of an audit is low. For example:

- ❑ We performed an audit very recently and there is little additional value that would be obtained by repeating the audit. Perhaps management is still in the process of addressing the issues we identified. There is no value in telling management and the board what we just told them.

- ❑ Management is aware of the issue and already has a task force (or equivalent) working on it. This was the case at Solectron with the issue of having too many factories with low utilization rates.

- ❑ The board and/or management are aware of the issue and an audit engagement would provide little objective insight. That was what happened at Maxtor with the inability of the engineers to design a new product that would make money.

- ❑ Another assurance function is addressing the issue and we would only duplicate their work, not add value. In this case, internal audit might assess the other function's approach and determine if it can rely on their work. There may also be an opportunity to partner with them, for example by lending audit staff.

- ❑ The risk is one that the external auditors are addressing and, as with another assurance function, there is insufficient value for internal audit to perform an audit.

- ❑ The board or management has engaged a third party, such as a consulting firm, to study the area. I would probably wait until such an engagement was over before considering an internal audit of the same area – and that audit would probably focus on areas not addressed by the consulting firm where the risk is high.

❑ The area is in the midst of change that would render any audit assessment obsolete. For example, the major systems might be in the midst of a major upgrade or replacement.

It is possible that the audit committee might tell the CAE not to perform an audit in a particular area. But the chances of that are, in my experience, remote. If it were to happen, I would have to wonder whether management wants internal audit not to perform the audit and has persuaded the audit committee that internal audit, for example, does not have the capability or expertise to be effective.

It is more likely that management will suggest that internal audit not perform an audit of a specific source of risk. Reasons for this can vary, from an honest belief that internal audit does not have the ability to add value because of limitations in their experience, etc., to a questionable desire not to have weaknesses identified and disclosed to the audit committee.

We will talk later about ensuring that internal audit has the capability to perform audits of any area of risk.

Assuming that we have filtered out any risks where an audit engagement would not add value, and the remaining risks are in priority order, we can start building the audit plan.

Is every risk "auditable"?

In early 2016, I was privileged to address IIA Sweden and then the internal audit team of a Stockholm-based bank. The continuing theme was that we need to focus our limited resources on the risks that matter.

I was asked this interesting question:

Are all risks auditable?

The question was asked after I had described some of the risks that we had identified at some of my companies, such as competitor risk at Business Objects. How can an internal audit engagement add value by 'auditing' such a risk?

The answer I gave is that we don't really 'audit' the risk. We are not in the business of second-guessing management decisions.

We are in the business of assessing the controls that are relied upon by management to manage the area of risk, including related management decisions and actions. We do that by:

1. Understanding the risk area and its related processes

2. Identifying the controls that management is relying upon to provide reasonable assurance that the risk is maintained at desired levels

3. Assessing the design of those controls

4. Testing and assessing the operation of those controls

5. Providing management and the board with our assessment of management's capability to manage the risk

The following questions about decision-making may help:

- Are the right people making the decisions?

- Do they have all the information they need to make informed, intelligent decisions?

- Is that information reliable, current, and timely?

- Have they consulted all relevant parties, including all those who might be affected by the decision?

- Do they have an appropriate understanding of risk levels and the effect their decision would have on risk levels?

- Do they have an appropriate understanding of the risk levels deemed acceptable, even desired, by more senior management and the board?

- Is there reasonable assurance that the actions necessary to support the decision will be taken?

These and similar questions can be used to assess the processes by which risks that matter are identified, assessed and evaluated, and treated.

For example, when we considered competitor risk at Business Objects, I looked at:

- Who was monitoring competitor risk in all its forms (e.g., changes in their pricing model or in marketing; whether major companies like IBM were acquiring our competitors; and so on)?

- Are they the right people, with the necessary contacts and network, intelligence if you like, to monitor and assess competitor risk – for all relevant competitors?

- Is their information reliable, current, and timely?

- Are they working with everybody required to address changes in competitor list?

- ...and so on

Earlier, I mentioned how I had conducted an audit of creativity and ideas (for marketing) at the Tosco Marketing Company. I considered the processes and related controls over:

- Who was responsible for identifying new ideas that could be used in marketing?

- Was there an appropriate process for encouraging and soliciting these ideas?

- Were all employees motivated to participate?

- Was there an appropriate, unbiased, process for evaluating all ideas?

- ...and so on

In this way, I was able to assess the system of internal controls relied upon by management to deliver useful ideas that could be used in marketing initiatives, delivering revenue to our convenience stores and gas stations.

I believe that we can make a contribution in this manner, assessing the controls relied upon to manage such non-traditional areas of risk.

## A dynamic audit plan

I am pleased to see a strong trend away from an annual plan to one that is updated as risks change.

When an annual audit plan is adopted, it is highly likely that audit engagements will address what *was* a risk at the time the plan was prepared – but which may not be a risk of the same significance now.

Risks change all the time. In fact, every business decision is likely to create new or change the level of existing risks.

So it is *critical* that internal audit operate with maximum flexibility, ready to change the audit plan as often as the risks that matter change.

But, maximum flexibility requires that internal audit *knows* when the risks that matter change.

As discussed in the last chapter, internal audit's first choice should be reliance on management's ERM. If that is not sufficient, internal audit conveys their assessment to the audit committee, works with management to upgrade the ERM to acceptable levels[35], and then performs its own risk assessment tasks as needed to build and then maintain the audit plan.

Dynamic audit planning changes the expectation from an annual plan that may be updated occasionally to a plan that may change significantly throughout the year.

The traditional approach is to spend a significant level of internal audit resources building a twelve-month plan.

But, when there is every expectation that the audit plan will change, perhaps significantly, that intense audit planning activity needs to change.

---

[35] *World-Class Risk Management* explains in some detail what I would consider acceptable quality. Basically, this is when management has reasonable assurance that new or changed risks will be promptly identified, properly assessed, and treated as necessary.

❑ Audit planning becomes a continuous rather than an annual activity. The end of the year is no longer the time to reset the audit plan; it may be the time to *reconfirm* the continuous planning process and support the annual budgeting process.

❑ The massive end-of-year audit planning process must change.

Rather than interview management and hold risk workshops over a short period, perhaps a month or so, it is better to spread the effort so that is year round.

It is essential to recognize that perfection is the enemy of being effective. We should be most concerned with what we should audit next, rather than what we should audit in a few months because it is likely that the risk universe will change again by then.

❑ I set expectations with management and the audit committee, so that they understand that my planning is flexible and will change as risks change. My reports to them indicate the more significant risks that I plan to address at some point, probably in the next twelve months, with an emphasis on those planned for the next quarter or so.

❑ Staffing of the audit department may have to change as each member of the department has to be involved, to a greater or lesser degree, in risk monitoring and audit planning – more on this later.

Some CAEs have tried to accommodate flexibility but stay with an annual plan. They include up to 40% of available time in the plan as "unscheduled" or "special projects", with the idea that should new risk areas be identified this bucket of unallocated time can be used for them.

But, this approach does not recognize that engagements that are included in the annual plan when it is presented to the audit committee at the beginning of the year may lose significance or value. In other words, while it may allow for audit engagements to be added, it does not encourage the removal of or significant change to audits on the plan.

It is far better to acknowledge from the beginning that the audit plan can change at any time. The goal is to perform audits of risk areas that matter now or will matter in the near future.

A flexible, agile audit plan

As I have said, my audit plan is flexible. In fact, I don't really have an annual audit plan at all!

I have a prioritized list of audits that can change every week. It might look something like the table below.

Each audit engagement is given a priority. "A" is a 'must do' project because of the level of risk (our initial assessment going in to the audit); because it has been requested by the audit committee; it is required by the regulators; or similar reason. A "B" project is close behind; it is less than mandatory, but seen as important. However, a "C" project is one that while it has value is not essential.

I endeavor to complete all "A" and "B" engagements and a fair number of "C" projects. However, there are years when I don't get to any of the "C's" and struggle to include audits relating to all the "B's".

You will see that the number of hours allocated to each engagement is small compared to what others may expend. That is because each engagement is focused on a limited number of risks, and always focused on what matters to the enterprise as a whole rather than the area being audited.

The last column shows the cumulative hours for the engagements to that point. I use this when I discuss with management and the board the level of resources I need. It helps them see what I can achieve with different levels of staff and co-source budget.

Audit Plan Example

| AUDIT PROJECT | Hours | Cumulative |
|---|---|---|
| A Cyber security - new data warehouses | 150 | 150 |
| A Employee business conduct training | 120 | 270 |
| A Compliance with revenue recognition rules | 200 | 470 |
| A Raw material inventory management | 200 | 670 |
| A ERM effectiveness | 300 | 970 |
| B Cash flow management | 120 | 1090 |
| B In-house app store | 100 | 1190 |
| B Reliability of spreadsheets used in FP&A | 120 | 1310 |
| B Capital investment allocation | 150 | 1460 |
| C Contracting with professional services firms | 100 | 1560 |
| C Fraud risk assessment | 100 | 1660 |
| C Advertising cost | 120 | 1780 |

This is a list of prioritized audit engagements[36].

For audit committee reporting, I may (but don't always) add a column that indicates in which quarter I am likely to perform the audit. But there is no other commitment about dates.

As each audit draws towards a close, I will discuss with the team (usually the audit director responsible for the area) which audit we should schedule to follow. At that time, we may adjust the planned scope (i.e., the risks to be addressed), staffing, and/or duration of the audit.

---

[36] The hours indicated are reasonable given my audit approach of focusing on enterprise risks rather than all the risks that are important to a location or business unit. When the audit engagements are short, the audit plan becomes more flexible and internal audit more agile.

We try to be flexible so we can perform each audit when it makes sense to do so, so it addresses risks that are important now, and so we can provide management and the board with the information they need when they need it.

At some of my companies, especially at Solectron, we needed to schedule audits as much as 60 days in advance. This was necessary so that management could ensure the appropriate personnel would be available to help with the audit. However, I resisted every attempt by management to persuade me to have a rigid schedule, with dates, for the full year.

Before closing this section, I want to mention a key word: agile. Internal audit needs to be agile so that it can address what matters, when it matters, in a way that matters. A key element is the flexibility to change plans and move to a different audit when the need arises.

The antithesis of agility occurred when I was with Business Objects and the company had agreed to be acquired by SAP.

I led the team that addressed integration risks – and they were huge. SAP decided, for good reason, that they wanted to move the Business Objects business from the existing Oracle ERP to the SAP ERP. That was fine, except they wanted to accomplish this in six months!

Anybody who has been through an SAP implementation knows that this is a high risk endeavor. Although both were software companies, SAP's business model was a relatively small number of high value sales. Business Objects had a large volume of small to medium (with a handful of large) sales. In addition, the way in which software maintenance was contracted for and billed was vastly different.

I was able to use my Business Objects team to staff the project, but I needed additional resources. SAP's risk management leader[37] lent me some of her top people and initially SAP's internal audit leader promised me his support. However, he had to back off that commitment because

---

[37] Miriam Kraus, the Senior Vice President for Global GRC at SAP, is a top notch risk management executive.

he had an annual audit plan that was anything but agile – any change had to be pre-approved by the CEO, and he was not prepared to request such a change.

Now let me put this into perspective. Business Objects was by far the largest acquisition that SAP had made (at that point and they haven't made any larger ones since). A failure to effectively integrate Business Objects could have had major implications on revenue, cost, and the SAP share price.

These days, business is moving at a great pace. Internal audit needs to be sufficiently agile to adapt and move alongside the business, rather than racing to catch up.

To quote Jack Welch, former CEO of GE:

"If the rate of change on the outside exceeds the rate of change on the inside, the end is near."

### Defining audit engagements that matter

The relationship between a source of risk and an audit engagement can be complex.

What I mean is that usually more than one area of risk may be addressed in a single audit, and it may take more than one audit to address all important aspects of a single source of risk.

In Chapter 2, I described how we had addressed the materials procurement risk at Solectron. We performed what were essentially multiple audits to assess whether that risk was being managed effectively: an audit of the corporate sourcing function; an audit of procurement at our Penang, Malaysia facility; an audit of procurement at our Suzhou, China factory; an audit of procurement at our Charlotte, North Carolina plant; and an audit of procurement at our Bordeaux, France location.

While I had the same team perform each of these audits, they didn't go immediately from one to another – if only to give the auditors time to recover from international travel. We also released separate reports for each location as well as one for the overall assessment of controls over materials procurement.

The combination of audit work for materials procurement was 100% operational. We didn't perform any work on IT-related controls. That was my decision. When we identified the key controls over materials procurement at each location, we assessed the risk due to a potential failure of IT processes to be relatively low.

That is a critical step: multiple controls are typically relied upon to address a single risk.

We need to assess the potential for an IT-related control to fail such that it would cause the overall system of internal controls to be less than adequate – in other words, such a failure would cause the level of materials procurement risk to rise to an unacceptable level.

Our assessment was that the key controls were manual. Although a failure in IT-related controls would be important, failures in bidding, contracting, and the general approach and attitude of the procurement staff were the main reasons procurement efforts would either succeed or fail. So, we did not audit related IT controls.

In 2010, the IIA published Practice Advisory[38] 2200-2: *Using a Top-down, Risk-based Approach to Identify the Controls to be Assessed in an Internal Audit Engagement*. Important sections of that Advisory include:

4. A system of internal control typically includes both manual and automated controls. (Note that this applies to controls at every level — entity, business process, and information technology (IT) general controls — and in every layer of the control framework; for example, activities in the control environment, monitoring, or risk assessment layers may also be automated.) Both types of controls need to be assessed to determine whether business risks are effectively managed. In particular, the internal auditor needs to assess whether there is an appropriate combination of controls, including those related to IT, to mitigate business risks within organizational tolerances. The internal auditor needs to

---

[38] I refer to a number of Practice Advisories in this book. The references are current as of September, 2016 but the IIA is in the process of replacing them with Implementation Guides.

consider including procedures to assess and confirm that risk tolerances are current and appropriate.

5.  The internal audit scope needs to include all the controls required to provide reasonable assurance that the risks are effectively managed (subject to the comments in paragraph 9, below). These controls are referred to as key controls — those necessary to manage risk associated with a critical business objective. Only the key controls need to be assessed, although the internal auditor can choose to include an assessment of non-key controls (e.g., redundant, duplicative controls) if there is value to the business in providing such assurance. The internal auditor may also discuss with management whether the non-key controls are required.

7.  The key controls can be in the form of:

    - Entity-level controls (e.g., employees are trained and take a test to confirm their understanding of the code of conduct). The entity-level controls may be manual, fully automated, or partly automated.

    - Manual controls within a business process (e.g., the performance of a physical inventory).

    - Fully automated controls within a business process (e.g., matching or updating accounts in the general ledger).

    - Partly automated controls within a business process (also called "hybrid" or IT-dependent controls), where an otherwise manual control relies on application functionality such as an exception report. If an error in that functionality would not be detected, the entire control could be ineffective. For example, a key control to detect duplicate payments might include the review of a system generated report. The manual part of the control would not ensure the report is complete. Therefore, the application functionality that generated the report should be in scope.

The internal auditor may use other methods or frameworks, as long as all the key controls relied upon to manage the risks are identified and assessed, including manual controls, automated controls, and controls within IT general control processes.

8. Fully and partly automated controls — whether at the entity level or within a business process — generally rely on the proper design and effective operation of IT general controls. GAIT-R discusses the recommended process for identifying key IT general controls.

9. The assessment of key controls may be performed in a single, integrated internal audit engagement or in a combination of internal audit engagements. For example, one internal audit engagement may address the key controls performed by business process users, while another covers the key IT general controls, and a third assesses related controls that operate at the entity level. This is common where the same controls (especially those at the entity level or within IT general controls) are relied upon for more than one risk area.

10. As noted in paragraph 5, before providing an opinion on the effective management of the risks covered by the internal audit scope, it is necessary to assess the combination of all key controls. Even if multiple internal audit engagements are performed, each addressing some key controls, the internal auditor needs to include in the scope of at least one internal audit engagement an assessment of the design of the key controls as a whole (i.e., across all the related internal audit engagements) and whether it is sufficient to manage risks within organizational tolerances.

Applying the Practice Advisory to the Solectron case, we identified the key controls as manual: at entity (global sourcing from Corporate) and activity levels (at each location).

The materials procurement set of audit engagements was not typical of our audits at Solectron. Most of the time, each audit engagement addressed multiple enterprise risk areas at a single location. In most cases, we also audited related key IT controls in that engagement.

For example, we might have identified the following as significant enterprise risks for which we needed to assess management's controls:

- ❏ Inventory management (ensuring sufficient but not excessive levels of materials to support manufacturing)
- ❏ Material inspections and quality management
- ❏ Customer invoicing and collections
- ❏ Physical security (primarily to address the risk of materials theft)

For each of these risks, we might have identified the key controls as functioning at each of our manufacturing locations (i.e., not at corporate), and that the greatest source of risk was at our larger facilities. As a result, our audit plan would include audit engagements at those larger facilities and focused on these four areas of risk.

Typically, the audit team for the audits of those larger locations would include IT auditors (or capable operational auditors), who would assess the IT-related key controls for those areas of risk. That was appropriate at Solectron because the IT environment was highly fragmented: each location had its own IT systems, maintained and managed locally.

At Tosco, Maxtor, and Business Objects we took a different approach[39].

The business process controls over risks were addressed in 'focused' audits. (What I mean by that is that the audits were generally focused (or, if you like, the scope of the audits was limited to) specific areas of risk. These audits were generally short, less than 200 hours in duration; I like short, focused audits as they are emblematic of a dynamic, flexible audit approach.

The IT-related controls were addressed through our routine IT general controls audits. As described in GAIT-R[40], the scope of our IT general

---

[39] Solectron had factories all over the world so almost every audit required at least some of the auditors to travel. It was more efficient to audit several risks in a larger single audit than perform the multiple focused audits that we did at my other companies.

controls audits was designed to address the controls within IT processes that provided reasonable assurance that automated (and semi-automated) controls function consistently as desired.

In other words, at these other companies, each risk that mattered was addressed by a combination of audit engagements – a focused audit of related business process controls, and (as part of the scope of) the IT general controls audit.

There was one situation at Business Objects that was a spin on the approaches described above. We had accounting service centers at each of our regional headquarters. A failure to perform controls properly at one of these service centers represented an enterprise risk that mattered.

Rather than have one team audit each location in turn, we decided to audit each location at the same time with the local audit staff. This enabled us to not only provide an overall, enterprise-wide assessment of the enterprise risk, but compare notes as we performed the audits.

Each audit benefitted as a result: when we saw what appeared to be differences, we could ask management why; when we saw what appeared to be a best practice in one area, we could immediately discuss it with management at the other areas; and, we took advantage of the local knowledge our local audit staff had of practices, language, and culture.


## Assurance or Advisory

The *Standards* and *Definition of Internal Auditing* talk about providing assurance and consulting (also called 'advisory') services. What is the difference? I distinguish the two types of service based on the end products and the primary customers.

---

[40] *GAIT for Business and IT Risk*, noted above.

Assurance engagements[41] are intended to provide a formal assessment of the adequacy of the controls management relies upon to ensure risks are at acceptable levels. The primary customers are the audit committee and top management. Secondary customers include operating management. In addition to the audit opinion, internal audit works with management to identify corrective actions as necessary.

On the other hand, consulting or advisory engagements[42] may or may not include a formal assessment by internal audit. The primary customer is most frequently operating management and the service provides insights and advice on how to ensure risks are managed as desired.

There is very often a considerable level of overlap between assurance and advisory services. For example, a typical (assurance) audit report will include recommendations or agreed actions (more on this later) – that might be considered 'advisory' as they are included to help management improve its processes and systems. Likewise, a consulting engagement such as a pre-implementation review of the controls and security of a new computer system should provide management with assurance that those controls and security will be adequate once the implementation has been completed.

The distinction I make is whether the primary purpose of the audit engagement is to provide assurance to the audit committee and top management, or to help management with advice and insight.

---

[41] The *Glossary* to the *Standards* defines assurance services as "An objective examination of evidence for the purpose of providing an independent assessment on governance, risk management, and control processes for the organization. Examples may include financial, performance, compliance, system security, and due diligence engagements."

[42] The Glossary to the *Standards* defines consulting services as "Advisory and related client service activities, the nature and scope of which are agreed with the client, are intended to add value and improve an organization's governance, risk management, and control processes without the internal auditor assuming management responsibility. Examples include counsel, advice, facilitation, and training."

Whatever you call an audit engagement, and it is too easy to get "hung up" over a name, I will use the results of both as input to my overall assessment of risk management and internal control.

I like the discussion in the IIA's 2006 Position Paper[43], *Organizational Governance: Guidance for Internal Auditors*. It makes an important point that is relevant to more than internal audit's governance-related audit engagements:

> In an organization with a less mature governance structure and process, the internal audit function may be focused more on advice regarding optimal structure and practices, as well as comparing the current governance structure and practices against regulations and other compliance requirements. In organizations with more structured and mature governance practices, internal auditors could focus more on:
>
> - Evaluating whether companywide governance components work together as expected.
>
> - Analyzing the level of reporting transparency among parts of the governance structure.
>
> - Comparing governance best practices.
>
> - Identifying compliance with recognized and applicable governance codes.

In other words, where management's processes and controls are less than mature, an assurance engagement may be of less value than an advisory project. Helping management upgrade an area that is known to have frailty is more useful than telling management what they probably already know – that the processes need improvement.

One reason that I like to distinguish an assurance engagement from an advisory project when I build the audit plan is because an advisory project will often consume more time and audit resources. While I can

---

[43] The Position Paper is no longer available from the IIA and considered by them to be out of date.

halt an assurance engagement as soon as I have concluded the assessment, an advisory project is likely to continue and help management identify the best path forward.

In *World-Class Internal Auditing: Tales from my Journey*, I tell the story of a pre-implementation review of a major systems project for the Tosco Marketing Company. I considered that an advisory project.

After my team shared with senior management their assessment that the likelihood of the system failing was high, the decision was made to go ahead anyway because the cost of a delay was higher than the level of risk.

My team continued their work, identifying specifically where the system would be most likely to fail and working with management to put precautions in place.

The system *did* fail, precisely where the team predicted, but management was ready with duct tape to prevent disaster and the implementation succeeded.

## The Scope and Objectives

Since we are talking about risk-based auditing, it is logical that the great majority of audit engagements, and probably all assurance engagements, will be focused on one or more specific enterprise risks. They may be limited to a particular location, business unit, or so on – but they will be focused on how activities at that location impact those specific enterprise risks.

For example, if we identify the procurement of materials as a significant area of risk, separate engagements might be added to the audit plan that focus on materials procurement in three locations: Sydney, Paris, and Ottawa.

If we also identify code of conduct training as a significant area of risk, where the delivery of training and related controls are local, we might include work relating to that risk in the audits we perform in Sydney, Paris, and Ottawa.

The scope and objectives for each of these three locations would then be:

The purpose of this audit is to review and assess the controls at this location over two areas of enterprise risk:

- Materials procurement

- Code of conduct training

An alternative way of expressing the scope and objectives could be:

The purpose of this audit is to review and assess the controls at this location over two areas of enterprise risk, to determine whether they provide reasonable assurance that risks are at desired levels:

- Materials procurement

- Code of conduct training

One of the 'arts' of audit planning is to address the many significant enterprise risks with a limited number of audits, combining the assessment of controls over multiple risks into each audit engagement.

At the same time, the planner must resist the temptation to add to the scope any areas of risk that are *not* significant to the enterprise but are considered important to that location.

I'm not saying that should never happen, but that the planner should be aware that every increase in scope to address a local risk may be at the cost of performing work elsewhere on a risk that does matter at the enterprise level.

I like to start every audit with a clear idea of the goal, what the end product will be. For assurance engagements, that will be an assessment (which I call my opinion[44]) as to whether the controls provide reasonable

---

[44] Curiously, the *Standards* do not require that every audit report include an opinion. Instead, they call for an 'assessment'. My view is that unless an opinion (or equivalent) is provided, the auditor is not providing the assurance that our stakeholders need. A list of deficiencies, or saying that there are no deficiencies, is not the same as a positive assertion that controls are or are not adequate to manage the risk.

assurance that the risk is at desired levels. Some might call that the objective of the audit.

On occasion, I have used a different technique to define the scope and objectives. This works best when the concern is more around the efficiency of the process.

For example, we had a situation at the Tosco Marketing Company where the process for approving requests for capital expenditures was taking so long that by the time the spending was authorized, the opportunity to obtain value from the spending had passed.

The alternative is to phrase the scope and objectives in the form of a question. The auditor's task is to answer this question:

> Does the authorization process for capital expenditures *meet the needs of the organization*, considering not only the appropriateness of the approval but the timeliness of the process?

That question, "does the process meet the needs of the organization?" helps focus the auditor on the core issue, the significant area of risk.

The question also makes the auditor ensure he or she understands what the needs of the organization really are! We tend to take that for granted. As a result, we may call something effective because it complies with documented policies and procedures, without considering whether the system is performing at the level required to meet organizational objectives. (See the story of the audit of Treasury in the section on auditing compliance in Chapter 13.)

I recommend considering a question to frame the purpose of your audit engagements.

For example, my recommendation when assessing the adequacy of risk management is to answer the question:

> Does the practice of risk management meet the needs of the organization, enabling better decisions and an improved likelihood of achieving objectives?

The Overall Opinion

I am a strong advocate that the CAE should provide a formal overall assessment of the systems of internal control and risk management[45] to the audit committee (or full board) and top management on an annual basis.

While some do not think this is necessary or even achievable, a growing number of governance codes around the world require internal audit to provide an overall opinion. I believe that in time this will be recognized as not only best practice but mandatory.

I started doing this in the mid 1990's at Tosco and have not looked back. The board very much appreciated the assessment, as did management.

I believe this is the primary value that internal audit can provide to any organization.

It provides leadership of the organization with confidence that they can rely on its people, processes, and systems to support their initiatives and achieve enterprise objectives.

It provides leadership with the confidence to *take* the risks necessary for success.

---

[45] I consider governance processes to be part of the systems of internal control and risk management. Technically, internal control exists to manage risk, so I could readily make the case that we should just be assessing the management of risk – but it is easier to talk about the more traditional view of internal control and how it helps manage the risks that matter.

There are some that believe internal audit should provide assurance on governance, risk management, and compliance (or control). I don't agree with this position. Internal audit can provide advisory services to help the board assess its practices, but I don't believe internal audit should put itself in the position of assessing the competence, integrity, or performance of either the board or executive management. Instead, I believe we should assess whether there are processes and controls in place that address the risk of ineffective governance. We can also share best practices in governance. But going further is a step too far, in my opinion.

An opinion on the overall systems of internal control and risk management does <u>not</u> mean that the CAE is opining on the management of *every* risk. It represents the CAE's professional opinion on whether there is reasonable assurance that the risks that matter, the risks addressed in the audit plan, are at desired levels.

Let me break that down.

An opinion is just that, an opinion.

As professionals, we are capable of forming and communicating our opinion.

Every professional provides an opinion. It's not a statement of fact, it's an opinion – and we are not only entitled to form but to share that opinion.

There is a possibility that we are wrong, but if we and our team perform the work to appropriate professional standards we should be able to stand behind it and provide an overall assessment of the condition of the controls over the risks that matter.

I argue that if we don't provide that opinion, we are shirking our professional responsibilities.

There's a huge difference in the quality and value of assurance provided by an overall opinion compared to the value of individual reports with opinions on the management of specific risks.

The overall opinion is clear, concise, and actionable.

When only individual reports are provided, the CAE is leaving the audit committee and management to determine for themselves whether, overall, the systems of internal control and risk management are adequate.

Why make them make that assessment, guessing whether deficiencies in one area mean that the overall assessment is that it is deficient?

I think the CAE should step up, take the risk, and share his opinion.

When I provide my opinion, it:

- Is formal, in writing

- Is an assessment of the systems of risk management and internal control over the more significant risks to the organization and its objectives, based on the work performed during the year; that work is reflected in the audit plan and reports on the audit engagements that have been completed

- Is based in part on the insights obtained by auditing by walking around, talking to management, and being present. The assessment is not limited to the formal audits that have been completed

- Is a positive statement, rather than a 'negative' opinion. The latter is where you point out the risk and control issues but don't make a positive assertion on the condition of the risk and internal control systems. I dislike the negative opinion as it makes the board and top management guess what our real opinion is

- Where there are risk and control issues that merit special attention, or where parts of the organization are of concern, they are highlighted

In other words, I try to provide the board and top management with the information they need if they are to understand the condition of the risk and internal control systems, whether risks are being managed at acceptable levels, and whether action is required by them.

For example, while at Tosco, I highlighted the issues at the Avon refinery in Northern California while praising the strength of the Bayway refinery in New Jersey. The contrast was especially useful to the audit committee.

I explained that controls over financial reporting were fine, but those over some operational risks were not. I told them what they needed to know.

My communication is intended to help the board and top management discharge their governance and oversight responsibilities. It is not about telling them how good we are and how successful we have been in identifying deficiencies.

I will talk more about the overall opinion in Chapter 9 and communicating to the board and top management in chapter 12.

Because my primary end product is this annual assessment, I design the audit plan to give me the input, the information about the management of risk that I need.

### Audits that MUST be included in the audit plan

In some organizations, there are regulations that stipulate that internal audit must perform certain work.

I am not talking about the *Standards*, which in some cases use the word 'must' when talking about audits of certain areas, such as governance. I believe that to be mistaken and have been working with the IIA's Standards Board for several years to have changed. The *Standards* are principles-based, including the principle that the selection of audit engagements should be risk-based. The *Standards* should not dictate that an audit must be performed in any specific area. Rather, they should dictate that engagements in defined areas should always be *considered* in developing the audit plan – and included therein when the level of risk justifies.

Leaving that aside for a moment, there are legal requirements for certain organizations that must be observed.

For example, when I was at Tosco, we were required by US regulations to audit our use of foreign trade zones[46]. The New Jersey team performed these audits every year that were reviewed by federal examiners.

---

[46] Foreign Trade Zones are explained by the US Department of Homeland Security: "Foreign-Trade Zones (FTZ) are secure areas under U.S. Customs and Border Protection (CBP) supervision that are generally considered outside CBP territory upon activation. ....they are the United States' version of what are known internationally as free-trade zones.......While in the zone, merchandise is not subject to U.S. duty or excise tax. Certain tangible personal property is generally exempt from state and local ad valorem taxes.....Goods may be exported from the zone free of duty and excise tax."

There wasn't a great deal of value to the company in performing these audits, but they were required. So, we did them with both speed and quality (including first class workpapers) – freeing up our time for the audits that were high in value.

The same applies to those in regulated industries, such as banking or insurance, where the examiners require internal audit to perform specific audit engagements. There is little to do except complete them fast and well.

Hopefully, the CAE has been successful in helping the audit committee understand the value when internal audit performs audits and consulting engagements on higher risk areas, so the audit plan is not overwhelmed with must-do audits at the expense of high value work.

## Organizational governance

In *World-Class Internal Auditing – Tales from my Journey*, I wrote:

> A failure in governance (and this extends way beyond the code of conduct) can be enormously detrimental to organizational success. Lord Smith of Kelvin[47] chaired the UK's Smith Committee on Corporate Governance that provided guidance to audit committees. He told the IIA International Conference in Kuala Lumpur that "the fish rots from the head down". Should we not inform the audit committee when the executive team is fighting with the CEO or among themselves, or when we see that the CFO does not have the confidence of his team and peers?

The authoritative studies into the causes of corporate failures and the Great Recession all point to weaknesses in organizational governance. For example, the report[48] by the Organization for Economic Co-operation and Development (OECD) said:

---

[47] Chair of the committee that wrote the Smith report on corporate governance in the UK, focusing on the role of the audit committee.

[48] *Lessons Learned from the Financial Crisis*

- This Report concludes that the financial crisis can be to an important extent attributed to failures and weaknesses in corporate governance arrangements.

- When they were put to a test, corporate governance routines did not serve their purpose to safeguard against excessive risk taking in a number of financial services companies.

- Potential weaknesses in board composition and competence have been apparent for some time and widely debated.

This should not be ignored by either risk or audit professionals.

In fact, governance-related risks may well be among the most significant areas of risk to any organization.

It is essential to include them in internal audit's risk assessment and audit planning, especially when there are indicators of problems.

The IIA has a set of standards around Governance:

### 2110 – Governance

The internal audit activity must assess and make appropriate recommendations for improving the governance process in its accomplishment of the following objectives:

- Promoting appropriate ethics and values within the organization;

- Ensuring effective organizational performance management and accountability;

- Communicating risk and control information to appropriate areas of the organization; and

- Coordinating the activities of and communicating information among the board, external and internal auditors, and management.

**2110.A1** – The internal audit activity must evaluate the design, implementation, and effectiveness of the organization's ethics-related objectives, programs, and activities.

**2110.A2** – The internal audit activity must assess whether the information technology governance of the organization supports the organization's strategies and objectives.

Now I have a problem with the *Standards* saying we **must** perform any specific audit[49]. I have voiced that concern on a number of occasions to the Standards Board, but making the necessary changes is not high on their list of priorities.

The *Standards* say that (emphasis added) "The internal audit activity *must* assess and make appropriate recommendations for improving the governance process".

What the *Standards* should say (and I believe the writers meant to say) is that internal audit must *consider* risk in these areas when building the audit plan.

*Considering* the risk is quite different from automatically including governance activities in the audit plan. If internal audit assesses the level of risk as low (for example, if they completed an audit in the last year that found the controls to be solid), there is no business case for an audit; there are better uses of internal audit time, addressing risks that matter more.

Leaving that aside, internal audit should recognize that most major financial statement frauds involved the active participation of both the CFO and the CEO. Further, when governance is weak, leadership, morale and performance are highly likely to suffer; sub-optimal goals and objectives are set; and so on.

In an article for the *Internal Auditor magazine* in 2012[50], I gave some examples of governance-related risks:

---

[49] Some IIA leaders have told me that when the Standard says "must assess" that does not mean "must perform an audit". Frankly, I cannot understand the nuances of that argument.

[50] *Auditing Governance Processes*, February 2012. I also joined Richard Chambers for a discussion for *IIA AuditChannel*[50].

- Organizational strategies are approved and performance monitored by executives and the board without reliable, current, timely, and useful information.

- There is too great a focus on short-term results without sufficient attention on the organization's long-term strategies.

- Oversight by the board is limited by a lack of directors with the required business, industry, technical, IT, or other experience.

- The board's dynamics do not include sufficient challenge and skeptical inquiry by independent directors.

- Oversight by the audit committee is limited by a lack of experience in financial reporting and auditing.

- The external auditors fail to detect a material misstatement because part of their global team lacks the necessary industry experience and understanding of relevant accounting standards.

- Board oversight of risk management is constrained by a lack of risk management experience.

- Strategies approved by the board are not linked to individual goals and objectives of managers in operating departments.

- IT priorities are not consistent with business and organizational priorities due to a lack of communication and alignment of goals and incentive programs.

- Employees do not understand the corporate code of business conduct because it is not in their native language or clearly explained to them.

I have experienced all of these situations. I have also seen:

- A dysfunctional executive team. In one case, the COO repeatedly showed disrespect for the CEO at executive meetings and refused to participate in board meetings. In another, each executive put their individual objectives ahead of the corporation's, kept information to themselves, and did not actively support corporate goals.

- A Legal department that was not sufficiently resourced to meet the needs of the organization. I saw this at two companies and each time management frequently went to outside counsel (in an uncoordinated fashion) to obtain legal advice. Sometimes, they relied on their own lay experience.

- A board that is dominated by and/or is unwilling to change the CEO or CFO.

Internal audit professionals should ask themselves:

- What could go wrong (and what needs to go right) in the governance processes at your organization?

- What is the current level of risk to objectives from each of these sources?

- Do you have a reliable gauge of the risk?

- What needs to be done where the risk is higher than desired?

- Has the board and/or a committee of the board (such as the audit or governance committee) been informed?

- How can you or your team help address the issue, bringing the risk back within desired ranges?

- Is an assurance audit appropriate or is an advisory/consulting engagement better?

There is no single, universally accepted definition of 'governance'. OECD[51] defines organizational governance[52] (and their definition is the one I prefer and find referenced most often) as:

> A set of relationships between a company's management, its board, its shareholders and other stakeholder. Corporate governance also provides the structure through which the

---

[51] The IIA's definition is: "The combination of processes and structures implemented by the board in order to inform, direct, manage and monitor the activities of the organization toward the achievement of its objectives".

[52] *G20/OECD Principles Of Corporate Governance* © OECD 2015

objectives of the company are set, and the means of attaining those objectives and monitoring performance are determined.

This is very broad – much broader than discussed by Standard 2110, which mentions only the code of conduct, performance measurement and monitoring, the oversight of risk management, and communications among the parties involved in governance.

Each internal audit department should define governance in a way that is meaningful for them.

I typically would include:

- The activities of the board and its committees, including their oversight of risk management, internal and external audit, the culture and ethics of the organization, and management in general
- The hiring and firing of executives and directors
- Shareholder meetings and relations
- The activities of the executive team as a whole
- Strategy-setting
- Objective-setting
- Performance management
- Organizational design
- The setting of compensation targets for executives and the board
- The Legal function
- The whistleblower line, investigations, and the code of conduct
- Internal audit
- External audit
- Governance of technology and the IT function

It is not enough to identify significant governance risks.

The even more difficult task is determining what, if anything, to do about them!

Some CAEs are reluctant to do anything at all. They fear angering the CEO or CFO, a 'career limiting move'. I leave it to you to decide whether this fear should prevent a professional from addressing a source of area of risk to the organization.

Another frequent objection is that the board will not support internal audit involvement in assessing or providing advice on governance. But, my experience is that when the CAE explains how internal audit can add value, the board will seize the opportunity.

For some sources of governance risk, a traditional assurance audit engagement will work well. For example, my team performed audits of:

- The code of conduct, focusing how it is updated; translated into the languages of each business location; maintained on the corporate and local intranets; communicated to all new employees with training, testing, and certification; and certified by management and employees at least annually. The audit may extend to certification by contractors and temporary staff, vendors, and others in the extended enterprise.

- The integrity of reports used by the board and executive management in decision-making

- The security of reporting provided to the members of the board in advance of board meetings

- The Legal function, typically in the form of an operational audit

However, very often[53] an advisory or consulting engagement will work better.

I believe the CAE can add significant value in a consulting capacity with respect to organizational ethics by:

- Reviewing (and drafting if necessary) the Code of Conduct

---

[53] In my experience, and in the IIA guidance, advisory engagements are more productive. They are not seen as adversarial, but as added value.

- Reviewing (and being a lead advisor in the development if needed) the training and certification processes for the Code of Conduct

- Reviewing or drafting the quarterly certification process, especially for executives and key employees

- Participating and chairing (if necessary) the Ethics Committee[54] (I did this at Tosco, Maxtor, and Business Objects)

- Otherwise providing advice and insight

The CAE can provide similar consulting services when it comes to other governance activities. For example, I have done the following:

- Advised the audit committee and its annual self-assessment process, including drafting the questionnaire used and compiling the results for the chair

- Developed training programs to meet the ongoing needs of the audit committee

- Helped develop and participated in the quarterly SOX disclosure and certification processes

- Facilitated the SOX internal control over financial reporting compliance process, including having the program manager report to me

- Participated in the board's IT committee, providing them with technical information security and related advice as needed

In Chapter 6, I talked about how an advisory engagement might be preferred when the area is relatively immature.

---

[54] Our Ethics Committee oversaw the development and maintenance of the Code of Conduct together with the processes for training, testing, and periodic certifications. We also met to review the results of investigations and recommend actions to the CEO. When I served as chair, it was more to facilitate the discussion than to make any executive decisions (taking care not to violate independence rules).

An advisory or consulting engagement may also be the better approach when the area is politically sensitive!

When I make presentations about auditing governance-related risks, I often use the metaphor of *Mission Impossible*. Because the risk to the auditor is high, it is advisable to consider carefully the approach that will be taken before accepting the mission. After all, in some cases we are auditing our own boss, the one who signs our checks.

Sometimes, it is possible to partner with the board (or a committee of the board). For example, as mentioned above I have helped the governance and audit committees with their annual self-assessments.

Another possibility is to partner with another department, such as Legal or Human Resources. I have worked several times with the HR team where we ensured their employee survey would include the questions necessary to assess the culture of the organization, the morale of employees, and their trust in leadership. The Legal department may, with internal audit as a partner, engage a third party expert to evaluate and compare current governance practices against accepted best practices.

Caution is always the key to any audit engagement where there is a possibility to identifying a governance weakness or failure. Partnering with Legal to obtain client-attorney privilege may be an option.

The risk to the organization of an internal audit that mentions problems at board or executive level is typically such that I prefer not to put anything in writing, with the possible exception of a note sent only to the General Counsel.

In fact, most of my reporting on governance issues is oral and not in writing.

Sometimes, the best way to communicate (see the chapter on Communications) is in one-on-one meetings.

At one company, we were able to see that the CEO of a division was not demonstrating trust in his executive team. Talking to him in his office, in a confidential and non-threatening way, helped him not only see the issue but resolve to correct it.

At another company, a one-on-one meeting I had with a member of the board surfaced a concern he and a few others had with the CFO. I discussed the matter with the CEO, who was aware of the concern and welcomed my thoughts and insights. A conversation between the CEO and the CFO, and then the CEO and the board members, were sufficient to address the board's concerns.

As I noted earlier, I am hesitant to provide an opinion on the adequacy of governance by the board or top management. Instead, I may assess the adequacy of the management of the risk of governance failures.

Caution is the key word when providing an opinion that may be perceived as judging your own boss!

## The Control Environment

I served on the IIA's Professional Issues Committee for six years. The committee was responsible for the institute's Practice Advisories and Practice Guides.

At one point, I was on two teams developing guidance on (a) assessing governance, and (b) auditing the (COSO) Control Environment[55]. I admit there were times when I wondered why we were developing separate sets of guidance for topics that overlap so much. But, we did.

The Control Environment includes many governance activities such as the operation of and oversight by the board. However, it also includes other activities that operate at multiple levels of the organization, such as hiring, training, and so on.

Both include the Code of Conduct (or equivalent), which is a critical element of any organization's system of internal control.

The Control Environment is described in the Executive Summary of the 2013 update to the *Internal Control – Integrated Framework*.

> The control environment is the set of standards, processes, and structures that provide the basis for carrying out internal control

---

[55] Practice Guides: *Auditing the Control Environment*, April 2011; Assessing *Organizational Governance in the Private Sector*, July, 2012

across the organization. The board of directors and senior management establish the tone at the top regarding the importance of internal control including expected standards of conduct. Management reinforces expectations at the various levels of the organization. The control environment comprises the integrity and ethical values of the organization; the parameters enabling the board of directors to carry out its governance oversight responsibilities; the organizational structure and assignment of authority and responsibility; the process for attracting, developing, and retaining competent individuals; and the rigor around performance measures, incentives, and rewards to drive accountability for performance. The resulting control environment has a pervasive impact on the overall system of internal control.

The COSO *Internal Control – Integrated Framework* has five principles relating to the Control Environment:

1. The organization demonstrates a commitment to integrity and ethical values

2. The board of directors demonstrates independence from management and exercises oversight of the development and performance of internal control

3. Management establishes, with board oversight, structures, reporting lines, and appropriate authorities and responsibilities in the pursuit of objectives

4. The organization demonstrates a commitment to attract, develop, and retain competent individuals in alignment with objectives

5. The organization holds individuals accountable for their internal control responsibilities in the pursuit of objectives

At least four if not all five of these are elements of governance.

So, in practice we can focus on governance-related risks and not worry about Control Environment risks – with one significant exception.

Principle #4 is critical. But it is not enough to "demonstrate a commitment to attract, develop, and retain competent individuals in alignment with objectives". Competent individuals must actually be hired, trained, and retained. In addition, actions are required should any employee fall behind expected performance levels.

My advice is to consider whether issues, such as setting compensation levels below market, are a pervasive source of risk to objectives. If so, and the internal audit team should be able to assess those risks (if not identified in the ERM program), then I would consider including related engagements in the audit plan.

## Auditing controls or transactions

There's a huge difference between an audit that tests the integrity of transactions and one that tests the design and operation of controls.

Finding that all the transactions are valid and correct does not mean that the controls management relies on are present and functioning.

When I lead training sessions for leaders of the SOX compliance function, I ask how many of them have had their homes burglarized in the last year. (It's rare that anybody says they have.) I then ask whether that proves that they closed and locked their front door every time they left.

I get many smiles.

Yet, many internal auditors compare invoices to receiving documents and purchase orders and draw the conclusion that the controls are effective.

That is not correct. There has been no test to confirm that the controls were performed, let alone in place.

Most of the audits my teams performed were designed to draw a conclusion about the system of internal control relative to specific risks. Therefore, we took care to examine and test those controls.

Testing data would not provide us the information we needed.

But, sometimes we were concerned with assessing whether the transactions were valid.

For example, when we found the controls over accounts payable to be ineffective at a couple of companies, we were concerned that individuals might have taken advantage of the situation to commit fraud. So we performed audits designed specifically to test transactions.

There is a huge value, as discussed above, in providing assurance that the controls are present and functioning. Testing data only provides assurance about that set of data. It says little about whether management can rely on controls going forward.

Testing data for risk monitoring has its place, but I perform very few audits where the objective is to provide assurance on the data rather than the controls over the data.

The difference between an audit of controls and an audit of data should be taken into consideration when designing the audit plan and each individual audit engagement.

### Support for the external auditor

Internal audit does not *have to* provide support for the external auditor, but in some cases it is a valuable use of corporate resources. As such, it merits the attention of the diligent CAE – who is focused more on helping the organization succeed than technical boundaries and theories.

Whether it involves spending a little more time on documentation and so on so that the external auditor can rely on internal audit's work, or providing direct assistance[56] to the external auditor, the value can outweigh the cost. There's a 'profit' to be made.

I prefer having the external auditor rely on internal audit's work to providing direct assistance.

When the external auditor relies on internal audit's work, we perform our own engagement, provide management with our usual assessment, advice, and insight, but we also enable the external auditor to reduce

---

[56] Direct assistance is where internal audit provides a staff member who works under the direction and supervision of the external auditor.

their level of effort. The scope of the internal audit work is based on *our* needs, which include but are not limited to those of the external auditor.

Internal audit may have to document its work slightly differently, expand the scope and even the hours required to meet external audit needs, and make the time for external audit review. But, those additional hours and their cost should be far less than the reduced external audit hours and fees.

After all, the cost to an organization of an internal auditor's time is far less than the fee it pays to an external auditor for the same amount of time.

When internal audit provides *direct* assistance, the net value is less because there is no internal audit assessment. The only value is the net fee saving.

It is, of course, critical to obtain assurance that the external auditors' fees are being reduced and to know by how much. Otherwise, how can the CAE know that this is a good business decision? All too often, I have seen audit departments who don't do that.

In either case, providing support to the external auditor should not be at the cost of failing to audit more significant areas of risk. If this would be the case, I would either not provide the service or obtain additional resources from the audit committee – justified by the external auditor cost reduction.

Supporting management's assessment of internal control over financial reporting

I am a strong advocate for internal audit performing the testing of key controls over financial reporting. I have a chapter on the topic in my book for the IIA, *Management's Guide to Sarbanes-Oxley Section 404: Maximize Value Within Your Organization*[57].

This is how I explained the benefits in that book:

----

[57] Available on Amazon and from the IIA BookStore

- Internal audit practitioners are experts in internal control and their experience and insights contribute to an efficient and effective Sarbanes-Oxley program.

- When internal audit performs testing on behalf of management, it is more likely to be relied on by the external auditors, and this can result in significant savings on audit fees.

- Internal audit can perform combined or integrated audits that include both Sarbanes-Oxley testing and non-Sarbanes-Oxley work. The total number of audits performed, each of which management must support, is reduced.

- When internal audit tests Sarbanes-Oxley key controls, they are more likely to be able to recommend process and control enhancements than if the testing is performed by management.

- Internal audit is charged with providing assurance and consulting services on all major risks, including the risk of poor controls over financial reporting. They might be obliged to review and assess management's testing if they don't do it themselves, at greater cost to the company as a whole than if they did the testing.

The chapter continues:

Each company should weigh the risks and benefits of internal audit involvement in Sarbanes-Oxley. These considerations should be given significant attention by management and the board:

1. It is critical that internal audit have the resources to meet its commitments as documented in the charter. Its ability to provide assurance and consulting services on the organization's governance, risk management, and related control processes must not be impaired to the point that it cannot address issues of significance.

2. Internal audit may not perform a management function. It must remain independent and objective, consistent with The IIA's *International Standards for the Professional Practice of Internal Auditing*. It can, as a consulting service, facilitate the Sarbanes-Oxley program and provide day-to-day project management. It

can also perform testing of key controls. However, the following are management functions that cannot be assigned to internal audit:

a. Responsibility for the Sarbanes-Oxley assessment and program. These typically rest with the CEO and CFO

b. Making decisions relative to the Sarbanes-Oxley scope and program design. Internal audit may make recommendations, but management should make the final decision in each case

c. Assessing whether a deficiency will be considered, for the purposes of management's assessment of ICFR [Internal Control over Financial Reporting], a material weakness. Internal audit should share its opinion, but the decision rests with management

d. Assessing the overall adequacy of ICFR

3. The decision should be based on what is best for the company as a whole, considering cost, risk, value, and the need to points in (2) above. While most CFOs and corporate controllers are interested in assigning the work to internal audit, and internal audit professionals would prefer the work to be handled by finance staff, both must put the interests of the company first.

Reference should also be made to a thought leadership paper from The IIA, *Internal Auditing's Role in Sections 302 and 404 of the Sarbanes-Oxley Act of 2002*, which was released on May 26, 2004. Key points addressed in the document related to assistance with testing include:

"It is management's responsibility to ensure the organization is in compliance with the requirements of Sections 302 and 404 and other requirements of the Act, and this responsibility cannot be delegated or abdicated. Support for management in the discharge of these responsibilities is a legitimate role for internal auditors. The internal auditors' role in their organization's Sarbanes-Oxley project can be significant but also must be compatible with the overall mission and charter of the internal audit function. Regardless of the level and type of involvement selected, it should not impair the objectivity and capabilities of the internal audit function for covering the major risk areas of their organization. Internal auditors are frequently pressured to be extensively involved in the full compendium of Sarbanes-Oxley project efforts as the work is within the natural domain of expertise of internal auditing." (Executive Summary)

"Activities that are included in the internal auditor's recommended role in supporting the organization in meeting the requirements of Sections 302 and 404 include:

- Project Oversight.

- Consulting and Project Support.

- Ongoing Monitoring and Testing.

- Project Audit."

"Ongoing Monitoring and Testing

- Advise management regarding the design, scope, and frequency of tests to be performed

- Independent assessor of management testing and assessment processes

- Perform tests of management's basis for assertions

- Perform effectiveness testing (for highest reliance by external auditors)

- Aid in identifying control gaps and review management plans for correcting control gaps

- Perform follow-up reviews to ascertain whether control gaps have been adequately addressed

- Act as coordinator between management and the external auditor as to discussions of scope and testing plans

- Participate in disclosure committee to ensure that results of ongoing internal audit activities and other examination activities, such as external regulatory examinations, are brought to the committee for disclosure consideration."

In the early years of SOX, internal audit had SOX "thrust upon them". Whether they volunteered or not, the majority of organizations asked internal audit to lead the design of the SOX program (i.e., the identification of key controls), the documentation of those controls and related processes, assessing the design and testing the operating effectiveness of the key controls, and acting as SOX program manager (PMO).

As a result, the great majority was forced to curtail their risk-based audit activities – they didn't have the resources to do both SOX and 'regular' internal auditing.

Then the pendulum swung. The appropriate uproar, not only from CAEs but also from the consulting and external audit community, led to the majority of organizations setting up SOX functions (generally within Finance) and freeing up internal audit to focus on risk again.

However, in the last few years the value of internal audit performing SOX testing (and, in some cases, taking PMO responsibilities) became apparent. Internal audit was given (at last) the resources to both perform SOX testing and risk-based auditing.

When internal audit is asked to perform SOX testing but not given the additional resources - requiring the CAE to cut back on the audit plan such that important areas of risk are not addressed - this needs to be discussed with the audit committee of the board. Their decision is final, but they should understand the assurance that is *not* being provided as a result.


Audits that add value
A few years ago, I was talking to the CAE of a major US retailer. He was very proud that his team had identified millions of dollars of savings for the company through audits of its vendors.

But when I asked, he told me that he had not done any work relating to how the retailer managed risk.

For me, this reflected a trend towards CAEs designing their audit plan with the intent that they demonstrate the value of internal audit. Providing assurance, advice, and insight into the management of significant risks to the organization was not the primary driver.

Examples of value-adding audit engagements include:

- Audits of vendors and contractors
- Audits of benefit and retirement programs
- Audits of compliance by customers with license requirements
- Searches for duplicate payments

I believe in value-adding audits, but not at the expense of providing the audit committee of the board and top management with the assurance, advice, and insight they need.

My approach is to consider engagements where we can add value.

If I have resources beyond what is necessary for assurance, then I will certainly strive to include work I the audit plan that will deliver value. If I can justify acquiring *additional* resources that will enable me to add value-adding engagements, then I will. In fact, I was very successful doing this in building the contracts auditing team at Tosco.

Sometimes, the value is so potentially huge that I will talk to management and the board about including it in the plan in preference to medium priority sources of risk.

But assurance, advice, and insight on the risks that matter always come first.

### Resources and the audit plan

There are some departments that only perform audits where and when they have the resources, including competent trained individuals, to do so. The audit plan avoids areas where they don't have expertise. For example, they perform very few IT audits because they don't have IT auditors; they don't audit engineering projects because they don't have engineers on staff; and so on.

At the same time, the audit plan is designed to utilize all resources available – the total hours in the audit plan match the number of audit hours available. For example, if the high priority projects require a staff of 5 and there are 6 internal auditors, work will be found to fill the remaining hours. (Note: this is unusual; most functions have more high-value work than they can do.)

I don't ascribe to that point of view.

I define the risks that merit our attention and then consider whether I have the resources necessary to perform the appropriate audits.

In other words, if there is an audit that really should be done, because it is an important area of risk and internal audit can add value, then I will do my very best to find the resources.

Sometimes, the CAE has the staffing (hours) but the available staff doesn't have the training or experience to do the work. Often, training is the best answer. For example, at Tosco I attended specialized training in derivatives from the New York Institute of Finance when our trading desk and the associated risks grew; My team and I attended Six Sigma training when Solectron adopted that methodology for its manufacturing operations; and I routinely sent my team to at least ten days of training courses designed to meet their and the company's needs[58].

My preference (in addition to training) is to design the staffing mix to address the enterprise's significant areas of risks. In other words, design the staffing based on the work that needs to be done, not the work that will be done based on the staff available.

Many CAEs are now hiring non-traditional auditors (people who have not come from an external auditing firm or an internal audit co-sourcing firm), and I did that quite a lot. I hired:

---

[58] All the members of the audit team, from the CAE down to administrative staff, need the training necessary for them to improve their skills <u>and</u> round out the department's needs.

- Smart people from the business, whom I would train as internal auditors

- Individuals with a specialization I would need on a continuing basis, such as highly technical IT skills (whom we trained in auditing), a certified environmental auditor, an auditor from a trading company, and a certified engineer

Sometimes, the best way to extend the available resources beyond the current staff is through co-sourcing – hiring consultants or contract staff to supplement the audit team on a temporary basis. Like many CAEs I made extensive, but focused use of this technique. (According to a 2010 IIA survey[59], more than half of the CAEs in North America use co-sourcing, but only 34% in Western Europe and less than 20% do in Asia-Pacific; my sense is that the practice has grown since then. In 2015, more than 70% of CAEs worldwide relied on co-sourcing for at least 10% of their work[60].)

Examples included:

- Using experts in 'white hat' hacking to perform penetration tests of our information security at Tosco

- Engaging a former chief procurement officer to assist with an operational audit of purchasing at Tosco's phosphate fertilizer subsidiary

---

[59] *Internal Audit Around the World – A Perspective on Global Regions*, from the IIA Research Foundation

[60] In fact, 40.49% of CAEs surveyed use third party resources for 10%-24% of their work; 14.17% use them for 25%-49%. (The data was obtained by the IIA for use in this publication from the CBOK 2015 *Global Internal Audit Practitioner Survey* (Altamonte Springs, Florida, USA: The Institute of Internal Auditors Research Foundation), Q512: Internal Audit Services from Third Parties, "What percentage of your organization's internal audit activities were performed by a third party in the last calendar year? (CAEs only)". Visit www.theiia.org/CBOK for more information.)

- Engaging the former operations manager of a trading desk to lead and then advise on our audits of Tosco's derivative trading activities

- Hiring a former Sales EVP to help with an audit of sales contract management at Solectron

We sourced these individuals from a variety of sources, including but not limited to several consulting companies and temporary agencies.

In addition to using co-sourced resources for specialized engagements, we also used them on occasion to 'backfill' staffing vacancies and so on.

Finally, I worked with management to build a 'guest auditor' program. This is where we borrow staff from management for a short period of time. They supplement the audit staff on a specific engagement where they add expertise and experience.

The value is not so much in terms of reduced cost, or replacing an internal auditor who can now work on another project because the guest auditor is not trained in internal auditing and will need close supervision and review of his or her work.

The value is in the increased quality of the insight of the audit team as a whole.

We used guest auditors on occasion at Tosco and extensively at Solectron. Management likes the program because the individuals involved obtain additional experience that is useful to their personal growth and contribution.

When the resource constraint is a matter of budget, then the first thing is to check that the audit plan is properly prioritized: I don't have audits planned where the risk and value are low unless they are mandatory (as explained above).

If there are important projects and I don't have sufficient budget, then it is up to me, as CAE, to work with the audit committee and senior management to either obtain the budget or accept the risk of not performing the audits.

As I said earlier, the decision of the audit committee when it comes to budget is final. But, it is incumbent on the CAE to explain the budget he/she needs to address the risks that matter with audit engagements that matter. See the simplified example below.

If the staffing needs to be increased, the audit committee should understand which additional audit engagements would be performed. The way I do that is to inform them which engagements can be completed with current staffing (those above the line in the example below) and indicate which additional areas of risk (those below the line) would be addressed with one additional staff member (or equivalent), two people, and so on.

## Audit Plan with Resource Limitation

| | AUDIT PROJECT | Hours | Cumulative |
|---|---|---|---|
| A | Cyber security - new data warehouses | 150 | 150 |
| A | Employee business conduct training | 120 | 270 |
| A | Compliance with revenue recognition rules | 200 | 470 |
| A | Sales contract management | 150 | 620 |
| A | Social media risk management | 200 | 820 |
| A | Raw material inventory management | 200 | 1020 |
| A | Security & controls over new wire transfer system | 250 | 1270 |
| A | ERM effectiveness | 300 | 1570 |
| A | Sarbanes-Oxley management testing | 1000 | 2570 |
| B | Cash flow management | 120 | 2690 |
| B | In-house app store | 100 | 2790 |
| B | Reliability of spreadsheets used in FP&A | 120 | 2910 |
| B | Capital investment allocation | 150 | 3160 |
| C | Contracting with professional services firms | 100 | 3260 |
| C | Fraud risk assessment | 100 | 3360 |
| C | Advertising cost | 120 | 3480 |

This is a very simplified example! At each of my companies, we completed 10-12 audits per person each year. This can be achieved when each engagement is focused on one or more enterprise-level risks.

My philosophy was to limit each audit engagement to 200 hours or less. Exceptions would be made for major initiatives, for example when the team was involved in assisting a new systems implementation with assurance, advice, and insight on controls and security.

Relying on other assurance providers

Internal audit is not the only function in many organizations that 'audits' an area of risk. Examples include:

- An environmental, health, and safety function
- The compliance department
- A quality department
- The external auditor
- Security services
- and so on

The CAE should determine the extent to which reliance can and should be placed on the work of these assurance providers.

There is normally value to be obtained:

- By relying on the work of other assurance providers, internal audit can free up resources for additional audits
- Internal audit benefits from the subject matter expertise of the other assurance provider
- Internal audit assesses the effectiveness of the other assurance provider and can provide objective insight and advice to improve its operations
- Duplicate work is avoided, minimizing disruption to the organization

The IIA has provided us with guidance in the form of Practice Advisory 2050-3: *Relying on the Work of Other Assurance Providers* and a Practice Guide with the same title[61].

Here are key excerpts from the Practice Advisory:

---

[61] An IIA Practice Guide typically provides more detailed recommended guidance than a Practice Advisory.

6.  The internal auditor should consider the independence and objectivity of the other assurance providers when considering whether to rely on or use their work. If an assurance provider is hired by, and/or is under the direction of, management instead of internal auditing, the impact of this arrangement on the assurance provider's independence and objectivity should be evaluated.

7.  The internal auditor should assess the competencies and qualifications of the provider performing the assurance work. Examples of competency include verifying the assurer holds appropriate professional experience and qualifications, has a current registration with the relevant professional body or institute, and has a reputation for competency and integrity in the sector.

8.  The internal auditor should consider the other assurance provider's elements of practice to have reasonable assurance the findings are based on sufficient, reliable, relevant, and useful information, as required by Standard 2310: *Identifying Information*. Standard 2310 must be met by the chief audit executive regardless of the degree to which the work of other assurance providers is used.

9.  The internal auditor should ensure that the work of the other assurance provider is appropriately planned, supervised, documented, and reviewed. The auditor should consider whether the audit evidence is appropriate and sufficient to determine the extent of use and reliance on the work of the other assurance providers. Based on an assessment of the work of the other assurance provider, additional work or test procedures may be needed to gain appropriate and sufficient audit evidence. The internal auditor should be satisfied, based on knowledge of the business, environment, techniques, and information used by the assurance provider, that the findings appear to be reasonable.

10. The level of reliance that can be placed on another assurance provider will be impacted by the factors mentioned earlier: independence, objectivity, competencies, elements of practice,

adequacy of execution of audit work, and sufficiency of audit evidence to support the given level of assurance. As the risk or significance of the activity reviewed by the other assurance provider increases, the internal auditor should gather more information on these factors and may need to obtain additional audit evidence to supplement the work done by the other assurance provider. To increase the level of reliance on the results, the internal audit activity may retest results of the other assurance provider.

11. The internal auditor should incorporate the assurance provider's results into the overall report of assurance that the internal auditor reports to the board or other key stakeholders. Significant issues raised by the other assurance provider can be incorporated in detail or summarized in internal audit reports. The internal auditor should include reference to other assurance providers where reports rely on such information.

It is easy to recognize the similarity between this guidance and the rules followed by the external auditor before relying on internal audit's work. That's not at all surprising, since we are in the same situation. There is value in reducing our level of effort by relying on the work of others, but before doing so it is prudent to verify that the others' work is of sufficient quality.

Following that principle, I have no problem if the CAE simply follows the guidance used by the external auditor.

While we are on that subject, it is worth noting that there is one area of risk where almost every internal audit relies on the work of another assurance provider: the risk of materially incorrect financial statements. I think this is a wise approach.

Let the external auditor perform the work necessary to provide the board and top management with assurance that the financial statements filed with the regulators are free from material error, and focus our limited resources on other areas of risk.

However, the CAE must be alert to indicators that the risk of an external audit *not* detecting material errors is increasing.

In most cases the risk of a poor audit, one that fails to identify material errors in the filed financial statements, is low. But, the CAE should not overlook the risk when it is clear that there are issues.

For example, over the years there have been a number of audit failures due to poor audits of overseas subsidiaries by an affiliate of the external auditor. In addition, the US Public Company Oversight Board (PCAOB) has consistently reported concerns about audits of companies with securities listed on the US exchanges.

When there are indicators of a higher level of external audit quality risk, the CAE should consider working with the audit committee to ensure that the risk is addressed.

There have been some high profile failures due to excessive reliance on other assurance providers. A couple of examples were in the United Kingdom with the internal audit departments of global oil companies[62].

In one case, internal audit relied on the Health, Safety, and Environment (HSE) department. In the other, internal audit relied on the work of a reserves accounting audit function.

In each case, the other assurance providers failed to identify and report significant issues. The first company experienced multiple, serious incidents (fires, etc.) that were blamed on poor practices that had not been detected by the audits performed. While the HSE department had been 'audited' by internal audit, that review did not identify the fact that few if any of the HSE audit staff had worked for another company and were only familiar with policies and practices (now found insufficient) that had been in place for several years. The HSE staff was not familiar with the more modern practices that other oil companies had adopted. The second company experienced a material misstatement of the financial statements that was not identified by the reserves audit team.

Audits of highly-technical areas represent a significant challenge for any audit team. If the audit is to be performed by internal audit staff, it is critical that the team has the experience, training, and the time to

---

[62] I don't have personal knowledge of this situation. I am writing about what has appeared in learned articles, newspapers, and the reports of investigators.

perform quality work. I often would either outsource the audit or supplement the audit team with subject matter experts.

If the audit is to be performed by another assurance provider, the internal audit team that reviews the competency and so on of that assurance provider also needs to be sufficiently competent to perform a quality review. Again, this may require outsourcing the review or adding a subject matter expert to the audit team.

One tool that may be useful is an *assurance map*. The IIA has again provided some useful guidance on this topic. Practice Advisory 2050-2: *Assurance Maps* explains that an assurance map starts with the key areas of risk and then identifies which assurance provider is responsible for auditing it.

An assurance map is useful in a couple of ways: it identifies potential duplication of auditing work and it identifies potential gaps – where no assurance function is addressing the area of risk.

The assurance map should be completed collaboratively with all other assurance providers. Few organizations look kindly on the waste of valuable resources when an area is audited multiple times!

An extension of the concept of relying on other assurance providers is when internal audit collaborates with those other providers with joint audits. Both relying on others and collaborating with them are forms of "combined assurance".

At Solectron, internal audit would perform engagements at the major factories, focusing on a variety of critical risks. However, those same risks at the same locations were often assessed/audited by other groups, such as the Quality function.

We worked with these other groups and sent a combined team to audit the facility. We agreed on the program of work, how we would measure results, and how our assessment would be reported to management.

In this way, we minimized duplicative audits, cut down disruption of the business, made more efficient use of corporate resources, and provided management with a single report rather than their receiving multiple reports that might have different and confusing assessments.

Commentary

Building an effective audit plan is an art more than it is a science.

The CAE and his or her team uses their understanding of the business to identify the risks that matter; which should be addressed through audit engagements; what type of engagements they should be (assurance or advisory); where the risks should be addressed (i.e., whether multiple audits of different locations or processes are required, perhaps at different times); and defines focused scopes for each audit.

Because the business environment, both the internal and the external contexts within which the organization operates, changes dynamically, the risks are constantly changing and internal audit needs to be sufficiently agile to ensure it is always addressing what matters <u>now</u> rather than what used to matter.

The audit plan includes the engagements that will support the CAE's annual assessment, delivered formally to the board and top management, of the effectiveness of the systems of risk management and internal control.

A *dynamic* and *agile* audit plan demonstrates to the board and management that internal audit has identified engagements that will deliver the valuable information they need: assurance that they can rely on the organization's people, processes, systems, and organization, together with advice and insight that will help them upgrade those systems as opportunities arise.

## Chapter 7: The audit team you need

Earlier, I said "design the staffing based on the work that needs to be done, not the work that will be done based on the staff available".

That is where I start: what needs to be done?

Then I can start thinking about the team I need to perform the audits with a high level of quality.


### The need to think

I ask a great deal from my team.

I need them to THINK.

Thinking is not, sad to say, something that every internal auditor does.

In fact, most auditors are trained NOT to think! They are told to 'follow the audit program' and do what they are told. Sometimes, they are even told to do the same work as the last time the area was audited.

As we know today, the risks of today are very often not the risks of yesterday. Doing the same audit means we are auditing what *used to be* the risks, not necessarily what they are today.

While I would always prefer to hire people who have never been trained to "do what I tell you and follow the audit program", that is not always possible. Very often, I can see in the interview process who has the capability of thinking for themselves. If they have high potential, I will hire them and unlock their chains by insisting that they always use their intelligence. If they drift towards following the same program as last year, I ask them why – and persist until I get *their* answer, not an answer provided by somebody else.

If we are to gain **insights** and provide management with meaningful, valued assurance and advice, I need auditors who can:

- Think

- Imagine what might be

- Suggest options for improvement that management has not considered

People can be trained in technical matters such as auditing skills. They can learn the business. But, it is much harder to learn to be imaginative or to think logically.

As long as individuals have intelligence and their curiosity, imagination, and creativity can be unlocked, they have the potential I am looking for.

It takes an unusual recruiting and interviewing process to identify individuals with high potential. It takes a manager who acts more like a mentor and teacher than a supervisor to help those individuals further develop and realize that potential.

I am proud that I have been able to staff my teams with individuals who can think, are willing to challenge traditional thinking (whether by the business, internal audit, or me), and suggest creative solutions to today's and tomorrow's challenges.

They have told me, even people who have worked for me for years (or decades, in one case), that I have always challenged them.

One key is to never answer a question – if at all possible. Instead, help the questioner find the answer themselves.

Ivy Yeo worked for me at Maxtor and this is what she had to say on this topic:

> "You are the best teacher in my life! You just know when is the time to give me a straight answer to my question (for questions which are beyond my ability to solve). You know just when is the time to answer my question with another question to stretch my ability to think further and discover the answers on my own."

As a child, I learned the value of a short word: "why?"

In my 2$^{nd}$ grade math class, Professor Taylor asked the class a very simple question: "what is the square root of 4?" I put my hand up, but when I said the answer was 2, the learned professor asked me "why?" He made me think. Answering that this is what I had been told, or that 2 X 2 = 4 was not sufficient. He made me think through and come up with an explanation that demonstrated my understanding of the mathematics involved.

As a manager of people, I also use this simple question. It doesn't matter whether the individual has the right answer or not. I want him or her to explain to me *why* it's the correct answer.

### Experience

I ask, no I *require* my people to form and share their professional opinion (or assessment).

I need people with the experience necessary to form and express that opinion. That experience will generally include some combination of:

- Business experience
- Auditing experience
- Technical knowledge
- Inter-personal skills
- Judgment and common sense
- Leadership

The *number* of years is not always a good indicator of the *quality* of experience.

Many people who profess, according to their resume, to have (say) ten years of experience only have one year's experience, repeated ten times!

The combination of people in the team must have between them the experience needed to perform the engagements on the audit plan.

### Business experience

A successful and effective auditor has to not only understand the business, but what it is like to manage a piece of the business.

We cannot strive for nor expect perfection – only what is reasonable and achievable. The systems of risk management and internal control can only ever provide *reasonable assurance* and the auditor needs to understand not only what is happening within the context of the business, but what a reasonable person should expect (in the language of the US regulators[63], "*such level of detail and degree of assurance as would satisfy prudent officials in the conduct of their own affairs*").

It takes a certain level of business experience to be able to judge whether management's management of risk is reasonable or not. Just because something is possible – and there are always opportunities to improve business processes and controls – does not mean that it makes business sense to make those changes.

I have learned to ask this question: "what would you do if you were the manager in charge of this area?" It is very effective in making the auditor apply their experience and form a business judgment.

I accept that the auditor is taking a risk when he or she judges whether something is acceptable. Many would prefer to raise the issue (as a "finding") and let management decide whether to make a change. While I consider this to be "passing the buck" and failing to exercise our own professional judgment, I accept that where the issue is unclear, the auditor should have a discussion with management and collectively decide whether the issue merits taking action.

In *World-Class Internal Auditing: Tales from my Journey*, I tell a story that illustrates this point.

> I was with a large savings and loan company (very similar to a mid-size domestic bank). After a few years in their internal audit department, leading among others the IT audit team, I had moved into IT management with responsibilities that included information security. Randy, one of my former IT auditors and a gentleman that I had hired and thought well of, was performing

---

[63] In their 2007 *Interpretive Guidance* for management's assessment of internal control over financial reporting (i.e., SOX), the SEC quoted this language from the Foreign and Corrupt Practices Act of 1977.

an audit of our information security program. He met with me to review his preliminary findings.

Randy told me that we had a serious control weakness in that we didn't change the phone numbers people used to dial into the data center. They needed to be changed at least once every quarter; otherwise there was a risk that over time the numbers would become known by hackers.

I agreed with Randy that changing the phone numbers reduced the risk that they would be compromised. However, as I pointed out, once somebody called the number they had to provide a userid and password. They were at the gate to the castle, but needed a key to open the front door. After three attempts, the userid was locked. In addition, changing the phone numbers frequently had three results: first, users would write them down and keep them in an easy-to-find location – a security issue; second, users would forget the number and be unable to do their work without calling the security help desk for assistance; and third, all of this carried a cost that was probably higher than the value of any risk reduction.

The risk reduction would be minimal because even after somebody was able to dial in, enter a valid userid and the correct password for that userid, they needed to get past additional security defenses. They had opened the front door of the castle but there were still a portcullis to navigate and additional doors to each of our systems and databases. The operating system (IBM's VM system) demanded a second userid and password. To enter an application, access a data base, or perform other functions, required at least one more – a third – access authorization.

I explained to Randy that the dial-up number was only the prelude to needing at least three additional levels of authorization before being able to steal data or damage our systems. In addition, I showed him an article about a tool used by hackers to automatically dial phone numbers until they detected the tone from a network modem – indicating a dial-up connection; the hackers could find out phone numbers even if we changed them! He agreed but said that changing the phone number was necessary.

By now, I was starting to lose my patience. I had hired Randy because he had a good combination of technical knowledge and common sense. Why couldn't he see that this was a silly recommendation? So I asked him why it was necessary.

Randy's answer: because a book by a notable IBM expert said you should change your dial-up phone numbers at least quarterly! Instead of using his common sense, he was relying upon advice from somebody who had no knowledge of our environment, the risks, and the costs.

I asked Randy to go back to his manager, a very experienced IT audit director who had been hired from outside the company to take my old job. Unfortunately, that individual told Randy to keep the point in. It was only taken out after the head of internal audit saw my response to the audit finding that explained how there was little to no risk but significant potential for business disruption and cost by changing phone numbers frequently.

Why didn't Randy use the common sense I knew he had?

When I asked him whether he would change the phone numbers on a regular basis if he ran information security, he showed obvious discomfort. He referred only to the book, which had been given to him by his new manager.

He wasn't being allowed to think.

He wasn't being allowed to exercise his judgment.

He was doing what he was told, not what he believed was right.

The recommendation to change phone numbers did not make business sense. Instead, the audit team created a lot of work for IT management before the CAE brought his common sense to play.

We should never recommend something we would not do ourselves. But, we need a certain level of experience to be able to make that judgment.

Auditing experience and technical knowledge

While I place a value on auditing experience, it can be taught to intelligent people. It is easier to acquire than the ability to think for yourself.

If you want to hire people with specialized skills and knowledge, you may have to make accommodations on auditing experience.

If I want to add a specialist in manufacturing operations, cyber security, or sales contracting, I am unlikely to find one with much internal audit history. I would rather hire a great specialist with ten years running a manufacturing line and teach them internal audit than somebody with five years in both. The ten year specialist will have a deeper and broader level of understanding that can be valuably applied to an audit engagement.

Training can be useful, but can never be to the same standard as several years doing the work.

I place tremendous value on line experience – actually running a piece of the business. Not only is this relevant experience that can help the auditor understand what they see, ask the right questions, and provide valuable insights and advice, but they understand the challenges that management faces every day.

When I was a new internal auditor (albeit with ten years of external audit experience), I had the pleasure of working for an excellent CAE – Patrick Sheehan. When he reviewed my work, he thought that while my comments and assessment were accurate, they made no accommodation for the constraints on management of the area. He insisted that I thought through how I would act if I took over responsibility for the area, with the existing budget limitations, workload, and so on.

Patrick gave me a card to place in a prominent location in my office, where I would see it every day. That card, which I still have in my office, had one word on it.

When managers ask for my advice on how to advance their career as an internal auditor, I strongly suggest that they leave internal audit and spend some time as a line manager. That experience, which I had before I became CAE, makes anyone a far more effective internal auditor. It gives you empathy.

Before leaving the topic of experience, let me tell you that the average experience (business and audit) on my internal audit teams was about 18 years[64]. While I had some with less, they made up for it with their intellect, curiosity, and interpersonal skills. They had the confidence and ability to gain and share valuable insights and advice – as well as provide our stakeholders with their professional assessment of the condition of risk management and internal controls.

## Interpersonal skills

Perhaps the best way to explain my thinking on interpersonal skills is through contrasting stories.

At one time, I had an individual (XYZ) working for me as an IT auditor. He was technically strong and led a number of audits of computer operations.

We had built a strong, cooperative relationship with IT management, including with the managers and supervisors in computer operations. We had not only *talked* about helping them upgrade their systems and

---

[64] I emphasize my "internal audit" team, because I had other groups reporting to me – more on this later.

processes, but *demonstrated* through our work that we shared the same goals of helping the company succeed.

So, when the Vice President for Computer Operations (Murray) appeared at my door, I was pleased to see him – at least for a few minutes. I liked Murray, a plain-spoken and driven manager who always put the company first.

After a few minutes of greetings, he told me that we had a problem.

He appreciated that my team and I in general were committed to working with him and his team in a collaborative yet objective fashion. We didn't play "gotcha" like other auditors he had worked with in the past.

But, he was not sure about XYZ.

One of his supervisors had come to him, concerned that XYZ had a "hidden agenda".

Whenever XYZ talked to him, he felt that XYZ was hiding his real purpose – leading the supervisor to feel that XYZ could not be trusted. The supervisor was inclined to hide information from or at least not volunteer information to XYZ.

On reflection, Murray said he realized he had the same feeling about XYZ. He wanted to trust XYZ, as he did me and the rest of my team. But he was not sure that he could trust XYZ to be objective, fair, and balanced in his reporting.

This was not easy for Murray to say. It demonstrated his desire to work with internal audit and to act before our relationship began to suffer a lack of trust.

It took a while for me to get to the bottom of this. It turned out that XYZ had a style of interacting with others where he felt he had to appear "macho". By the way, this is not my interpretation, it is his; he said that he was raised to act this way in his native country and he could not change.

In the end, XYZ and I agreed he needed to move on. His interpersonal style was not conducive to building the kind of relationship I desired with those we audited.

Let me contrast this with a story about Katie Vo.

Katie worked for me at Maxtor and then at Business Objects. Like a few others I have had on my team (such as Laura Morton Natlich from my Tosco days), Katie has the gift of a warm and welcoming personality with the smile to match.

Initially, we were having problems with the external audit team at Maxtor. I was losing my patience with their unreasonable and unnecessary demands. Fortunately, most of their requests for information were in Katie's area.

She was able to build, in very short order, a trusted relationship with them. They were greeted with that famous smile and an obvious interest in them as individuals, not just as the external auditors. Whether junior auditors or experienced managers, the EY team became comfortable working with Katie and our coordination with them benefitted hugely as a result.

Katie was responsible for the Sarbanes-Oxley assessment and testing of controls managed by the accounting and tax departments. For whatever reason, the tax staff always seemed to be late in completing their work, while the accounting team often appeared to be confused.

The small lady with the large personality was again able to build relationships of trust. Everybody was happy to talk to her. They came to her whenever they had questions and were open when she needed information from them.

Inter-personal skills are not limited to being able to communicate clearly, listen actively, and so on. Those are all important, but even more so is the ability to build *trusted relationships* with those on whom we depend – and that includes the managers and staff of the departments we audit, at all levels.

If we are to be believed by our customers when we say that "we are here to help", they need to see it in our eyes, hear it in our words, and experience it in our actions.

As the leader of the internal audit team, I can make a personal assessment of each individual on my team. But, the true and only valid test is through the eyes of my customers.

When they tell me that they value my people, trust in them and their judgment, and appreciate their contribution to organizational success, then I know the team members have the inter-personal skills I cherish and demand of them.

### Judgment and common sense

As the saying goes, "common sense is not that common".

Common sense from internal auditors is, unfortunately, also not as common as it should be.

Common sense is subordinated to "this is the way we have always done internal auditing", "I had to follow the audit program", or "this is the way I was taught".

Common sense dictates that we use our *judgment* to determine what we should do, how we should assess the condition of risk management and internal control, and so on.

Judgment is something we need to learn to trust: our judgment and that of all those who work for and with us.

If we can't trust their judgment, then something is seriously wrong.

If we are to provide internal auditing services that matter, we need people whose judgment and common sense we trust.

Some CAEs and managers have a real, significant problem letting go and trusting their people. Two stories illustrate how this can lead to dire results. One was uncovered by an audit, the other I heard about from individuals who had worked for the manager.

At Tosco, a manager that I had known and liked for several years, and who was well thought of by management, was appointed to lead the commercial accounting function at one of our refineries. However, within a year or so problems started to emerge.

The most obvious was when his team billed the trading company on the other side of a commodity swap contract $6 billion.

The company used these contracts to hedge the price of its refined products, locking in the sales price it would obtain, with the other side (the counter-party) locking in the price it would pay to buy the products.

In a commodity swap contract, the two parties are placing opposing 'bets' on movements in the price of that commodity. Product doesn't actually change hands even though each writes a contract to buy/sell with the other (i.e., there are two contracts, one to buy and one to sell). Instead, one party will pay the other the delta between the contract price and the market price at the time specified in the contract. The company that was owed money would send an invoice for the other to pay.

However, commercial accounting billed the counter-party the *gross* amount of the contract rather than the net (I.e., the difference between the values of the two contracts). So, instead of sending an invoice in the thousands of dollars, commercial accounting sent one in the billions.

We were about to start an audit of this area, so we took this into account as we planned the work. This is how I described the audit in *World-Class Internal Auditing: Tales from my Journey*:

> When we asked the manager of the accounting group why his team had made an error, he said it was because HR would not give him the budget to hire people with a CPA. He was forced to get the job done with people who not only didn't have a CPA but may not have gone to college. This put an immense burden on him, because he had to insert himself into every activity. He was overloaded, tired, and mistakes will happen.
>
> My team told me this and I asked them what they thought about the staff this manager had working for him. Were they as inept as he said?
>
> Absolutely not, they insisted. Although they didn't have the CPA certification, they had many years of experience in this type of accounting and a deep understanding of the business – deeper than the manager!

My team went back and asked a few more questions. The staff told them that they didn't believe the manager trusted them. He gave them tasks but never explained why he wanted something done. So they never really knew whether what they had done was right. The manager kept all information about the business and its activities to himself; they did the best they could, but morale was low and they were all looking for other jobs.

The manager confirmed what they had said. He didn't trust them beyond performing tasks to his detailed instructions. He kept all decisions to himself because he was the only CPA, the only one qualified and trained to make the decisions.

This was tough. It was clear to me that the manager was the problem. ....He either had to change or go.

I met with the CFO and then the CEO of the business unit. They decided to let the manager go.

The manager was an excellent technician, had good presentation and related skills, but was not a good manager of people. He was blinded by the lack of certifications instead of using his common sense to see that they were perfectly capable.

The second story is of a CAE whom I similarly liked and respected – until I heard about this.

The CAE's team, like so many, was responsible for testing the key controls relied upon for Sarbanes-Oxley compliance. While she had implemented some leading-edge practices for the internal audit work, the manager she relied on to lead the SOX work had adopted a questionable approach.

Instead of spreading the testing over the year, or at least performing some of the testing in the third quarter, the manager directed that all the SOX testing would be performed in the fourth quarter. As a result, walkthroughs to confirm the design and documentation of the controls were not done until October and testing of the many controls by a few staff was compressed into a few months.

The burden on the staff was huge, requiring them to work as many as ten or twelve hours each day. Even then, they couldn't keep pace with the aggressive schedule set by the manager.

When they asked for additional resources (which would be co-sourced), they were criticized instead of heard.

Each year, the company got through the SOX assessment, but each year it lost its SOX staff.

Unfortunately, the CAE would not give credence to the staff complaints, even when she saw them all leave.

I believe she and her manager not only failed to lead the team effectively, but did not use common sense or exercise judgment in planning the SOX work.

As CAEs and managers, we are hugely dependent on the people on our team. It is easy to forget that they are the ones doing the work.

If we are to have world-class internal auditing, we need world-class work from the team. And that is not obtained by beating them. It is obtained by treating them with respect, listening, leading by example, and helping them to grow and achieve their personal goals.

## Curiosity, imagination, skepticism, and more

While I have put interpersonal skills first, I could make an argument for putting curiosity and imagination at the top of the list of skills I look for in internal auditors.

Skepticism has its place as well. But it can be overblown.

Auditors need to have a healthy dose of professional skepticism. They cannot believe everything they are told without obtaining some level of evidence to support it. That holds even when the people providing the information are people they like and trust.

After all, most frauds are committed by trusted, respected, and well-liked individuals.

But it is dangerous to go too far with skepticism.

If an auditor not only distrusts but is seen to distrust the people he or she interviews, then he or she will in turn be distrusted. Everybody will be reluctant to talk to him or her because they feel the auditor has an ulterior motive and is only interested in finding fault.

It is important to build an atmosphere of mutual trust, where management believes the audit wants to help them and the organization succeed.

So a healthy dose but not an overdose of skepticism is needed.

While a measured dose of skepticism is required, I am not sure you can put a limit on the level of curiosity and imagination an ideal internal auditor will possess.

Auditors need to be curious and inquisitive, desiring to know as much as possible about the business and how it is run. Imagination helps them come up with ideas, which may seem to be out of left field to management, for improving the business.

If all an auditor does is obtain answers to a predetermined list of questions, he or she will miss the opportunity to see beyond the obvious, the operation of traditional controls.

For example, if she hadn't been intellectually curious and imaginative, I don't think Laura (in the story recounted earlier about the audit of the Treasury function) would have thought of taking more risk with overnight investments.

Another example occurred towards the end of my time with Tosco.

I was in an executive management meeting in Phoenix of the Tosco Marketing Company. The company president, Bob Lavinia, asked the team about progress on the annual advertising campaign.

The VPs of Sales and Marketing reluctantly replied that they had not made progress.

Why? Because they couldn't come up with anything new to say. If the advertising didn't say anything fresh and new, they wouldn't be effective.

Bob asked why there were no new ideas and the VPs didn't really have an answer.

After the meeting, I went to Bob's office and we discussed the issue.

This was a serious problem because the company operated its Circle K convenience stores and Union 76 gas stations in a highly competitive market with low margins.

If we failed to promote our brand effectively, there was a high likelihood that we would lose market share.

I suggested to Bob that I could perform an audit to see why the pipeline of new ideas was failing. He was surprised but gave me his full support.

I was able to find the problem (a failure to include the store managers, the people closest to the customer, in the search for ideas). But that isn't the point.

The point is that the curiosity and imagination of the auditor (in this case, me) led to a valuable engagement that delivered significant value to the company.

We need to let the entire audit staff think, use their judgment, and exercise their creativity and imagination so we can deliver the assurance, advice, and insight so valuable to the organization.


## Leadership

CAEs and, in fact, all internal auditors have to lead.

The CAE leads the team as a whole, but must also be a leader within and across the organization. While he or she may have a position of authority within internal audit, the CAE usually must rely on their ability to influence other business leaders – from operating management through executive management up to and including the board.

With respect to the audit team, the CAE:

- Sets the vision
- Ensures all staff receive the information they need about the organization, including its objectives, strategies and plans, and changes in leadership or direction

- Defines the strategies (and a longer-term plan may be needed if change is needed to the function that will take longer than a single year)

- Determines the structure and organization of the department, including making assignments where he or she has layers with managers, and determining where the staff should be located

- Hires the individuals required to perform the work with efficiency and quality

- Ensures the risks that matter are addressed by audit engagements that matter

- Is responsible for the assignment of individuals to audits

- Supports the team when assessing issues and assessments and discussing them with management

- Ensures he and the rest of the staff receive the training and obtain the experience necessary to be successful

- Serves as the mentor, cheerleader, motivator, supporter, and example to the entire team

- Provides guidance when necessary to help an individual or group of individuals improve their contribution

- Is sufficiently agile to change direction – that of the team and himself as an individual – when circumstances require it

- Represents the team with all other parts of the organization, from the board to the lowest level

- Ensures the team is up-to-date with the latest methods and tools

Unfortunately, according to PwC's *2016 State of the Internal Audit Profession Study*, boards and executives only rate 28% of CAEs as very effective.

As important as leading the internal audit team may be, it is equally critical that the CAE be seen as a leader within the organization – with the board, executives, and operating management.

The PwC paper identifies five areas where each CAE should consider taking action:

- Vision: "Develop and share a vision for your function, aligned to the strategic objectives of the business and determine what is needed to get there, including resources and technology."

- Talent: "Make certain your talent model can respond to the organization's emerging risks by mentoring and developing future business leaders and supplementing the core team with outside resources."

- Position: "Consider whether you are taking enough action to build your stature in the organization and creating a platform for executives to empower you."

- Communication: "Challenge whether you are communicating with enough impact to get the attention of your stakeholders and influence results."

- Business Alignment: "Build trusting relationships throughout the business to raise your level of engagement across the business."

Each of these five areas is important to the success of the CAE. Without an effective leader, the internal audit team is unlikely to be successful.

My additions to the PwC recommendations are:

a. It is critical that the CAE report, without undue interference from management, to the chair and other members of the audit committee (and other directors as needed).

   I have no problem with the CAE reporting administratively to the CEO, CFO, or other top executive, but that executive should recognize that their role is limited: the first duty of the internal audit function is to the audit committee.

   The executive supports the operations of internal audit by ensuring they are 'tuned in' to the strategies, plans (for example, the CAE should be invited to attend the CFO's staff meetings), and key decisions of the executive team, and are recognized as senior members of management.

If operating management, for whatever reason, starts to be obstructive, then executive management should act in support of the CAE.

The executive also should help the internal audit team obtain the necessary resources to fulfil their obligations to the audit committee. (The audit committee and not the CFO should 'own' the internal audit budget. The CFO should have input and be free to share his or her views, but should not be able to set the budget – the final approval of the budget should be by the audit committee.)

b.  The CAE has to build mutual trust with the chair and other members of the audit.

Both must have confidence in the other, able to share and discuss information without concern that what they say will be repeated inappropriately.

The CAE must take care not to abuse this position of trust, for example by informing the audit committee of serious issues without first informing senior management. Surprising top management is not conducive to productive relationships with them.

c.  The CAE also has to build mutual trust and confidence with top management.

This requires that the CAE not only *talk* about shared goals – the success of the organization – but *walk* that talk all the time.

The CAE must be fair and balanced with all communications, not just audit reports, and make it clear that he or she recognizes the constraints of the business.

Reports, assessments, and recommendations should be practical rather than idealistic. Perfect risk management and internal control is not possible; reasonable assurance in both areas is the target, and some level of risk is not only accepted but desired.

When senior management has trust and confidence in the CAE and his or her team, they are far more willing to listen to the insights and advice of that team.

If internal audit is to be effective, it must work collaboratively with management to arrive at a fair and balanced assessment of the management of risk and the performance of related controls.

Management can help internal audit understand when the appropriate (for the business) level of risk is being taken. Management should feel free to challenge any assessment by internal audit, provide its own perspective, and help internal audit reach the right conclusion.

Internal audit effectiveness also depends on its ability to collaborate with management in identifying whether and what corrective action is required when opportunities for improvement are necessary and appropriate.

In some functions, internal audit 'writes up' its 'findings', makes recommendations[65] to management, and then waits for management to respond. I see this as 'tossing the issue over the wall' and, as I will discuss later, it is not conducive to identifying the best solution to the problem. The better approach is to work *with* management to identify the appropriate corrective action.

d.  The CAE has to ensure that the whole internal audit team walks the same talk.

When audit staff act as if they are the corporate police, it makes it impossible for management to believe the CAE wants to be a partner and trusted advisor.

e.  We all work in a volatile, dynamic business environment. The executive team must be agile to maneuver the organization to achieve its goals, and the CAE must (a) help as necessary, and (b)

---

[65] Unfortunately, some internal audit functions believe (in error) that they should not make recommendations because their job is to 'find' the issues and management is responsible for fixing them. This type of internal auditing is generally seen as a policing function, not seen in a positive light by management.

ensure that the internal audit function is similarly agile and (c) is able to respond as conditions demand.

f.  While independence and objectivity are important, the CAE must always be willing to at least consider what appears to be straying from the core role of internal audit.

When it is in the best interests of the organization and with the prior approval of the audit committee, the CAE should be ready to step forward and take on other responsibilities.

As CAE, I have acted as chief ethics officer, chief compliance officer, chief risk officer, and also managed the IT quality assurance function. I was able to do so without impairing my ability to perform my core function as CAE because I was not making management decisions.

g.  The CAE must act as an executive of the whole business, not just the leader of the internal audit function.

If the CAE wants to be perceived as an executive with a seat at the top table, he or she needs to act that way all the time.

- When in public, act as an executive

- When visiting a subsidiary or business unit, act as a corporate executive

- Learn as much as you can about the operation of the business, what makes it successful as well as where the weak spots are

- Be willing to share your perspectives and opinions, your advice and insights, on the business as a whole – in the same way as any other corporate executive

- Show you are invested in the success of the organization as a whole

- Don't limit yourself or your team by always focusing on risk and controls. Talk about the business. Consider yourself a business person who has the responsibility of leading internal audit, but is not limited by a narrow view

The direct reports to the CAE, whatever their title, are also important leaders of the team and, with the CAE, of the function and of the organization as a whole.

When I was at Tosco, I developed a list of attributes of a 'model' internal audit CAE, director, or manager. Although the list is now nearly 20 years old, it remains as appropriate as ever. (My direct reports held the title of Director.)

---

### A Model Audit Director

- Respects all the members of the audit team and ensures them a conspicuous place at the management table

- Stands behind, not in front of the rest of the team. Leads from the front but takes credit from the back

- Represents all of us with senior management and knows what is happening at that level

- Spends 80% of his or her time on audits, 20% ensuring the team runs well, and 10% helping the CAE

- Has a balanced life

- Is the chairperson, mentor, and cheerleader for the team, not the *supervisor* or *manager*

- Gets out of the way, only helping when really necessary

- Knows the limits to their knowledge and the vast extent of their ignorance

- Recognizes that others frequently have a better answer

- Knows how to ask the right questions, rather than always having the (right) answer

---

- We, not I

- Is never satisfied

- Sees solutions, not problems

- Shares knowledge, empowering others, instead of trying to retain it as personal power

- Has authority through deeds, not position

- Needs and obtains the respect of the group

- Helps, assists, and coaches, but does not complain or denigrate others

- Sees everybody in the department as part of the team, and enjoys the success of all of its members

- Never puts down another team member

- Is private with rumor

- Leads with a smile

Not only did I develop and share this list with my direct reports, who each led a team in a region of the organization, but I held them to it. I expected them to behave this way. Fortunately, I had hired well and each was a leader.

An important element of leadership is hiring people who are willing and able to challenge you, and then listening to their wisdom.

It's not always easy to hear opposing points of view. It's also not easy to voice them to your boss! So, when my people express disagreement, whether slight or significant, I respect them for it and listen carefully.

Hard to believe, but I don't have all the answers! My people often have not only a different point of view, but may have greater insight.

It's in my own interests to listen and learn from my people, whether senior or junior.

But, it is quite possible to go too far!

When I joined Solectron some years later, I was impressed by the CEO. He was energetic and very much alive to the needs of his customers. He had led the company to continued revenue growth, leadership in the industry, two Malcolm Baldridge awards for quality, and a very high level of customer satisfaction.

The CEO believed, as do I, in hiring strong people as his direct reports and then giving them a lot of freedom to make decisions. Like me, he solicited their opinions and listened.

Unlike me, he let the situation get out of hand. His #2, the COO, consistently challenged him in front of others and showed a lack of respect[66]. People noticed not only the lack of respect but the fact that there were no consequences!

The CEO had lost control.

His decisions were often ignored. The COO publicly refused to attend board meetings, saying that they were a "waste of time". I was a helpless viewer as the executive team started looking out for themselves and their individual interests instead of working together as a team.

When the board tired of the dysfunction, they fired both of them.

The saying goes that everybody should be a leader.

An interesting piece published by the Wharton School of the University of Pennsylvania, written by experts from McKinsey Quarterly and Knowledge@Wharton, is entitled "Why Everyone in an Enterprise Can – and Should – Be a Leader[67]". It starts with this assertion:

---

[66] I did not observe this myself as I was not present at those meetings. However, multiple individuals who were at the meetings related the same story.

[67] The article can be found at http://knowledge.wharton.upenn.edu/article/why-everyone-in-an-enterprise-can-and-should-be-a-leader/

"Leadership doesn't just start at the top. Leaders can also be found at the bottom of an organization and at just about every place in between."

The authors build on the theme:

"Regardless of whether people are on the top line or the front line, they should explore ways to exercise their leadership potential to the fullest. That is the only way in which they can create meaningful working lives for themselves and the organization can get the most from their efforts."

I am a firm believer that not only is this correct, but every individual has an opportunity to lead – and I demand that they do so.

Look at this, where they quote Helen Handfield-Jones, an independent consultant on leadership talent strategy and co-author of the book *The War for Talent*.

"Everyone can exercise leadership by being an individual contributor at any level of an organization. What does that mean? Ultimately it comes down to looking for opportunities to make the world a better place. That sounds grand, but when people apply that idea to their work situations, it means having a vision of how your unit, or you as an individual, can be more effective and creative, go beyond day-to-day requirements, and energize others around that vision."

Isn't that a definition of an outstanding internal auditor: somebody who is always looking for ways in which the organization can improve, explaining that vision, and "energizing others around that vision"?

Everybody, from junior auditor to the most senior director or manager, should not only be looking for ways to improve the effectiveness and/or efficiency of the organization as a whole, but also contributing their ideas on how the internal audit function as a whole can and should improve.

But it takes leadership from the CAE and his direct reports to encourage everybody else to lead in that way.

157

## A few words about hiring

I have hired a lot of people over the years. While I am pleased to say that the great majority were a success, I have to admit to making mistakes along the way.

When I followed my own principles, as expressed above, I did well. But, from time to time I made these mistakes:

- I have been unduly swayed by an individual's certifications and prior experience (according to their resume).

  Just because somebody has passed all the professional exams you have heard of (and some you have not) doesn't mean they are competent to do the job you need done. Just because they have many years at an organization that has a great reputation doesn't mean that they made a huge contribution to gaining that reputation.

  They may be an excellent round peg when you need a square one.

  The individual who will succeed must fit in with the rest of the team (enhancing that team, not causing friction), the culture and style of the organization, and more. Someone who has been successful at one place may not be in another.

- A couple of times, I have allowed my better instincts to be set aside – usually because the candidate seems to bring a lot of experience and other assets.

  When my instinct is not to hire, I should listen. Sometimes, I did not.

- I have been impatient. Others who interviewed the candidate liked him or her more than I did. Because I needed to fill the position, I have hired the 'best available' even though I was not really persuaded they would be the *right* person to hire.

I have an unusual interviewing style.

It's unusual because I want to find out whether the candidate has all the attributes that I need, for real and not just on paper.

It's not easy to test people's imagination and creativity – their ability to think for themselves.

I like to use scenarios. I will describe a situation that I know the candidate will understand but probably has not experienced. Then I will ask them to tell me how they would handle the situation. What would they do and why?

There's typically no right answer, but plenty of wrong ones.

For example, I may explain a situation involving accounts payable for royalties. I recall one candidate asking whether there was an audit program. When I said that there was not and it would be up to him to develop one, he said that if I gave him an audit program he could follow it. Fail.

Another candidate asked if there were department policies that he could audit against. When I said that there were no formal, detailed documented procedures, he said that would be his finding and he would stop auditing. Fail.

I want to see how the candidate thinks. He or she doesn't have to come up with the same answer as me; I just want to see if they can use their imagination to picture what is going on, and their creativity to figure out an approach that might work.

You can't evaluate an individual's capacity to provide valuable insight and advice based on a resume.

I was influenced by an interview I had when I was a candidate myself for the position at Tosco. I was meeting the chair of the audit committee and he asked me what I read. It was a question out of the blue, one I had never heard being asked in an interview. When I told him about the kind of books and periodicals I read regularly, he asked me why I chose those.

He tested my thinking, as well as my intellectual curiosity.

## A few words about performance appraisals and firing

I hate annual performance appraisals. I am pleased to see more and more companies recognize that this should be a continual and not a periodic process. Members of your team need to know how they are doing *all* the time, not just once a year (or even quarterly).

I adhere to the philosophy that if you have to do an annual appraisal, nothing should be a surprise to the employee.

If you, as their manager, have done your job, they already know how they are doing: their strengths as well as areas for improvement.

Feedback to the employee must be honest, but it must also be focused on helping that employee succeed!

It must not be an iteration of their problems. It must be focused on improving their ability to contribute to the value provided to our customers. Honest praise should be given freely.

Where there are areas for improvement, we must be willing to step up and help them address them.

But, when those areas are serious and are not improving, we must be willing to take a different and more difficult path.

I have had to help people leave internal audit. Termination should be the last resort when people are not performing *for you* at the level you need, but could be of value elsewhere.

I have had staff that were average at best as members of my team, but were able to perform quite well as unit controllers and so on. That's a win-win.

Honesty can help people realize that they don't belong. They are not performing well enough to advance their careers. On a few occasions, I have helped people recognize that their future was not with my team and they left of their own accord.

Occasionally, I have had to put people through a formal Human Resources process, where they are given formal warnings and so on. Happily, the majority came through with the improvement needed.

A few did not.

The former CEO of GE, Jack Welch, was once asked what his main problems were running that giant organization. He gave a list:

1.  People

2. People

3. People

I regret every situation where I had to discipline and especially every time I had to terminate someone.

I look at them as failures on my part. If they were not able to improve, I failed them.

Perhaps my greatest weakness is that I am usually to slow to act when a team member performs below expectations.

Perhaps that is one my greatest strengths as well! I believe in everybody on the team and will do what it takes to make both them as individuals and as members of the team succeed.

## Commentary

However good the CAE is, however experienced, talented, and inspirational, he or she will be severely limited without the right team.

The CAE cannot do all the work, have all the ideas, and know everything there is to know.

In fact, if the CAE does not surround him or herself with the right team, all of his and his direct reports' time will be consumed reviewing the work of others – which is a horrible waste of everybody's time.

I have talked to internal audit teams where one or more managers are dedicated to reviewing working papers and re-writing audit reports. Others tell me that more than half of their total audit team time is spent on administrative tasks, such as workpaper reviews, answering review points and questions, writing and rewriting audit reports, and so on.

None of this adds direct value to our customers in management or on the board.

Isn't it better to have a team where this level of supervision and being supervised is not necessary?

Certainly, every CAE should have procedures to ensure an acceptable (or better) level of quality. But, when so much time is spent on non-value added rework, the problem is huge.

The Lean[68] methodology refers to rework as a form of *muda* ("waste" in Japanese) for good reason. While the concept originally was applied in manufacturing, the rework created when audit staff have to correct workpapers or rewrite an audit report can be very significant.

Every hour wasted on rework is an hour not spent auditing a risk that matters!

In fact, I prefer to surround myself with the best people possible, help them decide on a direction, provide them with the tools and resources they need (which may include my insights and advice), and then get the hell out of their way.

Rather than micro-manage, I prefer to have people around me in whom I have confidence and in whose judgment I trust.

Rather than review workpapers, I prefer to talk to them about their engagement, what they found, why they reached the assessment they did, how things went with the management team, what needs to be done – if anything – to improve matters, and so on.

While I often find myself spending a lot of time on audit reports, it is not to change the assessment as much as it is to understand what the assessment should be, how it can be crafted for impact and action, and how our results should be communicated to management and, if necessary, the board. There will be more on all of that later.

My job is to hire, develop, motivate, train, and empower the people on the internal audit team.

Their job is to help me lead the organization with valuable assurance on risks that matter together with ideas for improvement that are practical and will be seized on by management.

---

[68] Developed by Toyota, the Lean methodology was originally deployed in manufacturing operations to reduce waste and inefficiency. It has since been extended to include Lean Finance and even Lean Internal Auditing.

I have spent a lot of time on this chapter talking about the team and its leadership. Building and nurturing an effective internal audit team is an often-overlooked activity but is absolutely essential.

## Chapter 8: The tools you need

Of course, the best "tool" for any CAE is a high quality team. But, beyond that there are several other essentials that at least merit consideration.

### Information

To be effective, any internal auditor needs information:

- Information about the company and its condition, plans, strategies, risks, and so on – enabling the creation of an audit plan that performs audits that matter

- Information about changes in the organization, so the audit plan can be maintained promptly

- Information about each area being audited, so the engagement team can spend its time wisely, and also so the team can make suggestions for improvement that are practical and valuable

- Information about every control being audited, so its design and operating effectiveness can be assessed

The COSO *Internal Control – Integrated Framework* talks separately about information and communication, i.e., for that information to be communicated. Internal audit needs both to be effective.

There are several ways that internal audit, not just the CAE and his or her direct reports, but every member of the team should receive information that will contribute to their effectiveness:

- Attending meetings of the executive team. If the CAE reports to the CFO, then he or she should be able to obtain very useful information from those meetings

- One-on-one meetings with executives, not only the executive to whom the CAE reports, but executives across the organization.

  The CAE should meet frequently, monthly if not quarterly, with the CEO. The General Counsel is another individual with whom the CAE (and perhaps others in the department) should have frequent communications and discussions

- Meetings not only with the chair of the audit committee but with other members of the board

- Visits to each major location, using the eyes and ears to learn everything there is to learn

- Attending meetings of the Finance team where they review the period's results, comparisons to budget and forecast, and hear explanations for variances and trends

- Obtaining and reviewing the same information used by the management team to understand the operation. This includes not only financial results, but also operational information such as inventory levels, safety statistics, customer satisfaction reports, revenue pipeline, personnel turnover, intrusion attempts, risk management reports, and so on

- Reports designed specifically for the internal audit function. These might include information on the status of prior audit findings as well as analytics developed by or for the team to monitor risks, for example fraud risks

- Reading publications about the company's industry (I used to get the *Oil and Gas Journal*, for example), materials from the IIA and ISACA (magazines, blogs, *CAE Bulletin* and more), and publications related to specific areas of audit interest (e.g., *SC Magazine* for information about information security; *CPA Letter* for information about financial audit and accounting; *McKinsey Quarterly* and *Harvard Business Review* for insights into business and management; and *Enterprise Risk Magazine* for risk-related articles).

These should be routine, but every member of the audit team should always be seeking to listen, observe, ask questions, and learn about the business.

For example, while a tour of a facility by a senior manager is interesting, it can be more interesting to be escorted by a middle-level manager or line supervisor. These individuals are closer to the business and their perspective can be revealing.

I also like getting multiple tours from different people. For example, a tour of a factory by the general manager, by the manufacturing supervisor, by the finance lead (it can be interesting to see how much or how little they understand about the business), and the head of security.

At Tosco, the Marketing Company ran about 6,000 convenience stores and gas stations. It was fascinating to spend a few hours with the district manager as he drove from store to store in his area. The insights he shared and my ability to see operations through his eyes were revealing. Without this, I probably would not have realized the extent of the disconnect between the people in the field and those in the headquarters' ivory tower.

All the audit staff, not just the CAE and his direct reports, need a lot of information not only about the business but also about the internal audit department!

I believe in staff meetings. I held weekly meetings with my direct reports, they held weekly meetings with their teams, and we all got together once every month or so.

Staff meetings are an opportunity for me to share what is going on at the executive level and issues affecting the audit department and its plans.

They are also opportunities for me to hear from the rest of the team about local matters, for the team to share information among themselves, and for each person to step forward and lead us when they have insights that could require a change in our direction.


## Analytics

I have been a big fan of analytics[69] ever since I used them as a junior staff auditor with Coopers Brothers in London on the audit of the Hercules Powder Company.

The UK subsidiary, like its parent in the USA, manufactured a fairly wide range of chemicals in its plant, just outside London. Most of the audit

---

[69] I like the definition in Wikipedia: "Analytics is the discovery, interpretation, and communication of meaningful patterns in data".

work was conducted at its central London headquarters, near Marble Arch.

The audit was notable for a number of things, including that in my second year we suffered through a coalminers' strike that caused fairly frequent and widespread electrical outages; the electrical power was curtailed to preserve fuel and limit electrical supply to critical consumers, such as hospitals. I vividly remember huddling close to a window so we could continue to audit by the light of a somewhat silvery moon.

The first year I was on the audit was also the first year Coopers had the audit. Kevin Gilbert was the lead auditor, an audit supervisor at that time. I was on the audit team for three years (before I moved into the Computer Audit Group) and was the lead auditor during that third year. Kevin was by then the audit manager.

Kevin had developed a novel approach to the audit.

The company kept excellent statistics for each of its products, including volumes produced and related costs, inventory levels, volumes sold and revenues realized, and gross and net profit levels. Kevin built what we would now call spreadsheets, but back then were manually-developed tables to identify trends and apparent anomalies.

As the lead auditor in year three, I did the analysis myself. I already had a good understanding of the business, having visited the plant several times, observed operations, and performed inventory counts. The numbers gave me deeper insights into the business.

Talking to management about the trends and the decisions they made as they ran the business gave me confidence in the numbers and an appreciation of the challenges they faced. Discussions included such issues as how they decided which products to manufacture, how they understood and reacted to fluctuations in demand, and how they set product prices.

Another experience reinforced my belief in the great value of analytics.

In 1979, I was working for Coopers & Lybrand in Atlanta, on a six-month exchange program. One client was AT&T Long Lines, the long distance telephone service of the phone giant.

With the assistance of a junior auditor, my task was to audit the IT general controls at the data center located just north of Atlanta.

To cut a long story short, I developed software that analyzed the system logs on the IBM mainframes the data center used. The software reported incidents of program changes as well as instances where production programs failed in production ('abends').

My testing, combined with a thorough analysis of root causes, identified a serious problem.

Production programs, all of which ran in 'batch' mode (i.e., on a scheduled basis), would sometimes fail. The application programmer responsible for the program would be called in and tasked with fixing the problem, almost always after hours. (They referred to this as an emergency change.) After some level of testing, the programmer would apply the fix and the code would be migrated into production.

However, the program would fail the next day and the programmer would again be called in to identify the problem, correct the code, perform a test of the revised code, and then get the new code moved into production.

But, yet again the code would fail.

The sequence would continue, each time leaving the programmer more and more tired from lack of sleep, prone to making mistakes, and rushing to get home so rushing or even skipping the testing. The level of problems kept growing.

When I shared the results of my testing and my conclusions as to the root cause, management refused to believe me. They were sure that not only were the programmers performing the testing every time they made an emergency change, but the work was reviewed by a supervisor before the change was migrated into production.

To prove my point, I created a chart that showed, over time, the level of emergency changes and the level of program failures. Both were climbing with the current curve heading almost straight up.

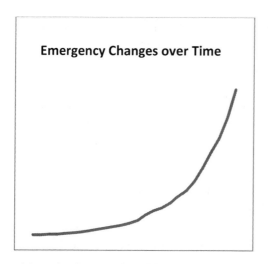

Emergency Changes over Time

This was persuasive. While my words were critical, they did not bring the point home nearly as well as a picture.

In today's world, analytics and charts can be developed much more easily. The software available to produce them continues to improve and is a great tool that can enhance many audit activities.

Analytics can help the audit team:

- Understand trends in the business. This information can be used when developing and maintaining the audit plan as well as prior to each engagement, to obtain a more detailed understanding of the activity being audited.

  Typically, when the auditor meets with management at the start of an audit engagement, he or she may ask the manager how the business is doing.

  But, if the auditor has reviewed the latest analytics, he or she can start the conversation by asking questions such as "I see your new products are not selling as well as planned; why do you think that is?" or "I noticed that the level of scrap and rework is much less this year; what are the main reasons for that?"

  The auditor not only has a better understanding that can lead not only to improved audit work (such as an improved ability to understand the root causes of both success and control failures) but also to an enhanced perception by management of their business knowledge and insight. This, in turn, can lead to improved relations and communications with management.

- <u>Understand changes in the business</u>. As discussed earlier, it is critical that the audit plan is updated as the business and its risks change. Internal audit needs to focus on the risks of today, not of yesterday.

- <u>Provide detailed insights into the operation</u>. Once the audit engagement has started, analytics that dive into operational details can help identify issues and opportunities.

For example, at Business Objects, my team based in Paris was working on an operational audit of the sales contracting process and the involvement of the legal staff.

The revenue recognition rules and best practice required a review by the legal team of all contracts. However, the attorneys were so busy on contract reviews that they were unable to provide support on other matters to management. As a result, management was either pursuing business opportunities without legal advice (not a risk the company wanted them to take) or engaging an outside firm that had much less of an understanding of the business and carried significant cost.

The audit team developed analytics (using the company's own software) that analyzed the level of contracts by size over time.

They were able to see that a large volume of sales contracts were very small in value. When they showed this to management and discussed the situation, their suggestion to have the legal team perform a reduced level of review on contracts below a threshold was well received.

The analytics not only helped understand the problem, obtain agreement on the solution, but also identified the threshold below which the legal review would be streamlined.

- <u>Improve the clarity and persuasiveness of audit reports</u>. In the same way, a chart or table in an audit report can provide valuable information much more clearly than words alone.

  However, auditors need to be judicious in the use of charts and tables. They should only be included where they add value and clarity to a point of information that the reader of the report needs. This will be covered further in a later chapter.

- <u>Assist with the detection of fraud and error</u>. Internal auditors have been using analytics to detect potential fraud and error for decades.

  I believe the primary responsibility for both the prevention and the detection of fraud, theft, and error lies with operating management. However, there are two situations where I believe internal audit should perform its own, independent search for potential fraud or error:

  a. In some organizations, the audit committee (probably at management's request) has assigned to internal audit some level of responsibility for theft and error detection.

     At Tosco, the Investigations unit for the Marketing Company reported to me. They used the same reports used by management, supplemented where necessary by analytics developed by the internal audit team.

  b. Where control deficiencies are identified that indicate an increased risk of fraud, internal audit may want to investigate whether individuals have taken advantage of the control weaknesses.

     This situation came up a couple of times that I can remember.

     The first was at Tosco, where an audit of accounts payable identified several serious control deficiencies.

     Bruce Taylor of the IT audit team partnered with the Investigations unit to develop a series of analytics programs in ACL. Bruce developed one software program for each area of risk, then one that consolidated the results of all the individual programs. The last identified where multiple risks could be seen in a single area, enabling the Investigations unit to focus first on those higher sources of risk. Fortunately, no frauds were identified.

The accounts payable function liked our software and asked IT to make it available to them to use as part of their regular process. IT decided not to support ACL (which is, after all, a programming language), rewrote the programs, and integrated them into their support of accounts payable.

The second case was at Solectron. Wendy Ng, a financial/operational auditor, was able to identify a serious weakness in the separation of functions around procurement and payables. The procurement supervisor at our Penang site had the access rights not only to create and approve a purchase order, but also to approve receipts and approve the vendor's invoice.

(As an aside, Penang IT management's response when Wendy brought the weakness to their attention was that they had a control in place. The control was that they did not tell people like the supervisor that they had additional access rights! It took some arm-twisting by me, but eventually management agreed that action was needed.)

Wendy used analytics to determine whether the supervisor had taken advantage of the control weakness. She was able to determine that the supervisor had neither approved a receipt or a vendor invoice.

I will cover more on the topic of fraud in a later chapter.

Before closing the discussion on analytics, I want to say a word about the question of when internal audit should develop its own analytics.

My strong opinion is that internal auditors' first choice should be to use the same reports and data that management uses to run the business. If those reports provide the information the auditors need, there are several advantages:

- There is next to no cost! The software already exists; the only task is getting added to the distribution list (if a report) or being given access (if an on-line report).

  Developing audit analytics, using software acquired by the internal audit department for their specialized use, takes one or more individuals with programming skills to spend a significant amount of their time developing and then maintaining the software.

  In addition, the audit software is not inexpensive – and consumes valuable internal audit budget dollars.

- The software is maintained by IT (in the great majority of cases) or by the user (occasionally). That means that when there is a need to update the software, for example if the structure of the database is changed, that update does not have to be done by an internal audit team member who may not (a) know of the need for an update, (b) have a thorough understanding of how to make the change, and (c) have the time to make the change.

  In fact, internal audit should recognize that every hour spent developing and then maintaining a program is an hour that cannot be put to valuable use on an audit engagement.

- Management's software runs in a secure environment.

  When internal audit develops its own software, they generally do not run it against the production database. Even when they do, or when they are able to run against a copy that they know has the same information, very often the first step is to extract the data to an intermediate storage location. The reason for this is that the analytics can take a fair amount of computer resource and IT would prefer that not be done in the production environment. That intermediate environment is likely to be less secure than the production environment.

- Management's software has been tested by both IT and the user. The risk of erroneous results is low. If internal audit uses analytics that are wrong, the results of the audit can be similarly wrong and the reputation of the department harmed.

- If internal audit identifies a problem with management's reports, or issues that management should have seen in their use of a report, this can be brought to the attention of management for their action.

- The data is subject to management's internal controls. Errors can be introduced if auditors extract and download data from the enterprise systems.

The second choice should be to use the same software that management uses but create a report just for internal audit. This can be done in a couple of ways:

a. Modify a program used by management. Sometimes all that is needed is to adapt an existing program. Perhaps a total is added, or an additional column of information. If the auditor wants only to see transactions over a certain value, he can modify a program that lists them all, simply excluding those under his or her threshold.

   Again, the cost is minimal. There is no need to buy software. Further, internal audit may be able to persuade IT to create the modification for them.

   If IT maintains the audit software, as before the impact on the internal audit budget is reduced. Similarly, the environment is more likely to be secure and the integrity of the results more reliable.

b. Develop a new program using the same tools as management. If the software is sufficient for management to use, why not internal audit? I am not talking about code written by programmers in IT, but software used by people like financial and operational analysts.

These days, most organizations have acquired Business Intelligence software such as Cognos from IBM, Hyperion from Oracle, or BusinessObjects from SAP. These applications enable users to develop reports using 'drag-and-drop' technology. They are easy to use.

If business users can learn to use this software, then I see no reason for internal auditors not to be able to do so as well. The software doesn't even require IT specialists to develop the reports. Financial and operational auditors can as well. Earlier, I mentioned that my Paris team at Business Objects used analytics in their audit of the sales contracting process. They used the BusinessObjects software without difficulty.

Again, the cost to use the software is minimal, especially when compared to the cost of acquiring software that will only be used by internal audit.

In addition, there are expert users within the business and IT that can provide support. Existing reports can be copied in many cases.

Business Intelligence and similar software is getting more and more powerful, easy to use, and accessible to users. Versions are now available on tablets and even phones.

Frankly, I believe all internal auditors should have a tablet and learn to use this software.

One of the problems facing users of specialized audit analytics tools (examples include ACL and IDEA) is accessing the database.

- IT may be reluctant to provide production access (often with very good reason) to a program that they did not develop or maintain.

  Frankly, they are right to deny such access as the risk is one they should not take. Instead, they will provide access to a copy or extract from the production system. Internal audit then has to obtain assurance that the copy they access is identical to the production version.

- Internal auditors, even IT specialists, do not have the same level of understanding of the structure of the database, how the different transactions are defined, and so on. Even though some of the software vendors provide 'interface' programs to help, they will not address custom fields and transaction types.

For example, SAP systems not only have multiple transaction codes ('t-codes') for credit notes (because that enables credits issued for different purposes to be distinguished), but the companies I audited added custom transaction codes for additional types of credit notes.

If the internal audit team includes programmers, they will figure out (with help from IT) how to access the database and deliver the data to the audit software. But, this can consume a lot of time and precious audit resources. Perhaps the specialists can be better used on an audit engagement!

- As mentioned earlier, there is a risk that IT will change the structure of the database in some way. They may not inform internal audit, who will continue to run their software without change, but now delivering incorrect results.

As an aside, when I was a young IT auditor with Coopers & Lybrand in the UK, one of my clients was the Guardian Royal Exchange. This large insurance company was based in Lytham St. Anne's, near Liverpool.

One of my tasks was to run test data against the company's INBR system (which calculated the reserve for claims that had been incurred but not recorded). The calculation was too complex to be checked manually and very hard to replicate with audit software. So, the audit team had developed a set of test data that the INBR system would analyze. If the system produced results that matched the predetermined reserve amount (i.e., what it should produce if it was working correctly), then the conclusion would be drawn that the company's calculation could be relied upon.

I provided the test data to IT management. They ran the software and provided me with the reports. The results were as expected.

But, as I reviewed the reports to make sure everything was run properly, I saw an old date for the version of the INBR system. Odd!

I asked management whether they had modified the INBR system in the last few years. They laughed and told me that it was being modified almost every quarter!

Stunned but somehow not surprised, I asked why they had not used the current system to analyze the test data.

The response was that they had diligently kept a copy of the version of the INBR system that was used for the very first test by the Coopers team so many years ago. Each year, they brought it back out – just for us, so we could have a successful test!

After all, the run instructions that the initial Coopers auditor had provided required that version of IBNR. They were just following our instructions. In fact, they told me, the format of the data had been changed several times and our old test deck would not work in today's environment.

There was no intent to deceive. Management simply did not understand what we were trying to accomplish, and the initial set of auditors (and those for every year since) had not thought to provide clearer instructions that specified that the same version of IBNR relied upon by management should be used in the test.

The last resort, in my opinion, is to develop custom analytics using software purchased by and only used by internal audit.

But, there is yet another problem – and this is huge!

World-class internal auditing requires a dynamic audit plan that ensures that all audit engagements are focused on the risks that matter today.

The risks that matter, and the audits that are performed, are generally not the same every year.

Software that is developed for a specific audit engagement (as opposed to software that helps monitor risks) may only be used once.

That means that unless the internal audit team is confident that there the same or similar audit will be performed in the future, the return on investment (ROI) for the software will be limited.

So much better to find a way to use management's reports and analytics!

An audit analytics team

I want to cover this separately because I see a number of larger internal audit departments establishing a team of specialists whose job is to provide analytics for the rest of the department.

The members of the team are usually a combination of programmers and IT auditors who are proficient in the use of audit software.

Mistakes I have seen include:

- Running the standard reports provided by the vendor
- Starting with accounts payable, receivables, inventory, and general ledger and developing reports that traditional auditors have used in the past. Examples include creating reports of potential duplicate payments
- Starting with the files and their content and developing reports that the team members' prior audit departments used

If the audit department's approach is to audit what matters to the organization today, it designs and includes engagements in the audit plan to address them.

The focus of the audit department is on risks.

But the audit analytics teams I have seen are disconnected from this approach and focus.

They are developing reports they think are interesting or know have been used by other audit functions.

What they need to do is provide analytics that meet the needs of the audit team they belong to: reports that enable that team and its members to identify and monitor the risks that matter and then assess the controls that manage those risks.

The risk-based approach MUST extend to the audit analytics team.

While reports that identify potential duplicate payments are interesting, the related risk is generally low[70]. There are better uses of everybody's time.

In fact, I would like the audit analytics team to provide tools and training so that every auditor can perform their own analytics at any time (especially if they have access either to mobile analytics on their tablets or to the company's analytics from their laptops).

The Business Intelligence tools are simple enough even for me to use.

The specialists can ensure access to the tools, the database, train new employees in their use, and assist those with more complex requirements.


Other tools

A host of other software is available, at a price, for internal audit departments. This includes:

---

[70] At Solectron, my predecessor as VP of internal audit had one of his staff develop ACL reports that identified nearly $1 million in potential duplicate payments. We ran that again after I took over. When I shared the results with the CFO he showed no interest. A million dollars got a ho-hum reaction. Then I realized that this was a $16 billion revenue company and the CFO had bigger issues on his mind.

- Audit management software, used to build and maintain the audit plan. The software may include features such as resource management, a staff skills database, automated working papers with remote review capability, issue tracking and follow-up, help with the audit report, and more

- Although less common these days, stand-alone software for some of the features typically included in audit management software packages, such as automated working papers

- So-called GRC software. I say 'so-called' because the software will usually be limited to functionality for risk management, internal audit, and (perhaps) compliance management and policy management. Other aspects of GRC such as strategic planning are rarely included.

  The functionality included for internal audit is typically the same as in audit management software. That is not surprising, as most of the software was originally designed for internal audit and functionality for risk management was added to reach the wider (and better-funded) market.

  In a GRC package, there may be an option to integrate the enterprise risk assessment with the audit plan. However, the enterprise risk assessment may be at too high a level to be easily integrated (audit engagements may be at the risk source level, while the enterprise risk assessment is for the organization as a whole)

  GRC software is an opportunity for an internal audit department that has next to no budget to obtain software because management is willing to purchase the software for risk management and other groups.

  However, I have seen a number of situations where the justification for the purchase of a GRC package is the value it represents for risk management; yet the internal audit team's evaluation of the audit management features results in a sub-optimal solution for risk management being acquired.

- Stand-alone software for such as:

- o Flowcharting
- o Issue management
- o Project management
- o Working paper management
- o ...and more

I am a traditionalist when it comes to using audit software. That means that I am a big fan (not surprising, since I developed quite a lot as an IT auditor) but at the same time I am selective and want to make sure I spend the department's limited resources wisely.

I strongly believe that the first step is to understand what you need and its value.

If you are a small internal audit department, there is little value in software for resource management and not much more in project planning.

If you are committed, as I am, to dynamic audit planning where you only plan at most a couple of months ahead, software that enables a detailed annual audit plan may take more time to maintain than it is worth.

Similarly, some departments will find little value in automated working papers or the ability to review them remotely.

As I said, the key to a successful choice is to identify which capabilities provide the greatest value and then the selection should be of the software (and that may be a combination of products) that best meets those needs.

Analyst firms, such as Gartner and Forrester, evaluate software products. They tend to focus on the so-called GRC solutions rather than on standalone products. As a result, their evaluations are based on the combination of functionalities *they* have deemed most important. That combination includes capabilities outside internal audit, often quite unrelated (such as policy management).

The analysts' ratings are interesting for their comments and can help identify options. But each internal audit function should evaluate alternative solutions based on their *specific* needs.

## Commentary

Every craftsman needs tools. But they have to be the tools that meet their needs.

Certainly, every auditor needs a lot of information to be effective and the CAE and his or her management team should make it a priority to enable all their staff.

Software and analytics in general can make a huge difference to the capability, efficiency, and effectiveness of an internal audit function.

The wise CAE monitors advances in the technology that can help his or her team. For example, it is useful to understand the new field of 'data science', defined in Wikipedia as "an interdisciplinary field about processes and systems to extract knowledge or insights from data in various forms, either structured or unstructured, which is a continuation of some of the data analysis fields such as statistics, machine learning, data mining, and predictive analytics, similar to Knowledge Discovery in Databases".

I am personally very interested in 'predictive analytics', whose purpose is to take current and historical data and project what might happen in the future: 'risks' and 'opportunities'. 'Machine learning' is also fascinating.

However, care should be taken to spend the department's limited budget on functionality that provides true and demonstrable value. Too many acquire software and only use a limited portion of its functions.

But the greatest tools of any internal audit function are the people on the team: their intelligence, curiosity, imagination, and insight – together with the ability to communicate their insight and influence change.

I am encouraged by the number of CAEs that I see providing training in these essential 'soft' skills.

## Chapter 9: The audit opinion

Internal auditors are paid for their professional insights and opinions.

While some complain that internal auditors' opinions are often subjective, and say they should only share what can be proven by objective facts, I heartily disagree.

My approach is to provide an overall opinion on the management of risk and the effectiveness of internal control – with respect to the risks that matter. I also provide an opinion with every individual audit engagement.

I don't understand people who say they provide assurance but won't share their assessment or opinion. A list of issues is *not* assurance.

When I was on the IIA's Professional Issues Committee, we developed recommended guidance on internal audit opinions[71]. For some reason that I cannot understand (all I know is that some members in some countries do not believe an opinion is always possible), the *Standards* do not mandate the expression of an opinion – either overall or after each engagement.

Yet, how can internal audit be said to be providing assurance if it does not share its opinions – its assessment of the quality of management's systems, processes, organization, people, and controls?

Corporate governance codes around the world (with the US noticeably absent) mandate internal audit opinions on the management of risk and the effectiveness of the system of internal control. In time, the IIA will catch up.

In the meantime, I have been providing both overall (what we called 'macro' opinions in the IIA guidance) and individual audit ('micro') opinions for as long as I have been a CAE.

---

[71] *Formulating and Expressing Internal Audit Opinions,* Practice Guide, March 2009

As I mentioned earlier, I build the audit team and plan so I can deliver the macro opinion.

Below is a sanitized version of what I shared with the Tosco audit committee in 1997. It was marked as 'attorney-client privileged, prepared at the direction of the General Counsel' because of the critical assessment of certain operations. I have included only the general introduction (Purpose and Assessment) and the Tosco Marketing Company sections.

## GENERAL AUDITOR'S ANNUAL REPORT

### Purpose

Each year, Internal Audit completes an increasingly large number of audits in areas considered to present the greatest risk to the company. The volume of opinions is such that it is difficult to see the big picture and assess the overall adequacy of controls. Furthermore, Audit does not review every area every year.

This report presents an overall, confidential assessment of the systems of internal control, including a comparison with the prior year where applicable. It is based upon:

- The results of internal audits completed during the year

- Any controls deficiencies reported by Coopers & Lybrand or other third party auditors or examiners

- Prior audit results, and corrective actions taken and reported by management

- The results of special and other projects performed by the department, and

- The personal observations of the Audit Department's management team

The company's General Counsel has requested this information, in anticipation of litigation.

The assessment is by division (and further if necessary) and by category of control objectives. Internal controls (as defined by the Committee of Sponsoring Organizations of the Treadway Commission) "are designed to provide reasonable assurance regarding the achievement of objectives in the following categories:

- Effectiveness and efficiency of operations [including the safeguarding of assets]

- Reliability of financial reporting

- Compliance with applicable laws and regulations"

## Assessment

The numeric scale used here is an admittedly subjective assessment of the risk presented by the control system. It is based on a combination of:

- The probability an adverse event may occur and not be prevented or corrected quickly

- The impact such an adverse event may have on the company

- The scale is from 1 to 5, where 1 is Low Risk (i.e., excellent) and 5 is High Risk (poor)

## Tosco Marketing Company

Effectiveness and efficiency of operations

| | | |
|---|---|---|
| - | 1997 | 3 |
| - | Change from prior year | None |

Reliability of financial reporting

| | | |
|---|---|---|
| - | 1997 | 1 |
| - | Change from prior year | None |

Compliance with applicable laws and regulations

- 1997                                         3
- Change from prior years              None

**Explanation for Ratings:**

The major reason I have a higher than desirable risk rating for the efficiency and effectiveness of operations continues to be IT. The systems inherited as a result of the acquisition of Circle K are by no means state of the art. One problem is that we don't know what we sell in each store, just what we purchase. This makes it difficult to target our marketing efforts, which include stocking each store with the right quantity of the right goods, and maximizing the effective use of our advertising dollars. In addition, TMC has more people than optimal; that is necessary until we can implement more effective systems. Our audits have found that departments are reasonably efficient given the limitations of the systems.

- Complicating this are three issues: (a) the process for managing change to our systems is not only fragmented but also does not provide adequate assurance that the changes necessary for effective business operations will be implemented with the required quality- especially important when the problems with program and data security are also considered; (b) the IT department has more staff that are average at best than we can afford, especially given the significant number of system conversions and migrations - let alone any new functionality that should be introduced; (c) the level of turnover within IT is much too high, and it is especially troublesome when good people leave.

- While I have confidence in [IT management], these are massive problems that will not be easily solved.

The 3 rating for compliance relates to the risk from inappropriate personnel-related actions by a manager in the field. While training has been developed and delivered, the risk remains.

Two decades later, I would modify this report to specify the corporate objectives where the level of risk is greater than desired. I would also include an assessment of the management of risk – not something many people were addressing in any formal fashion in 1997.

However, I believe this report provided the quality of useful information that was needed by the board and top management. Certainly, they found it useful and it sparked an excellent discussion among the board and with management (who agreed with the assessment).

If you are puzzled by the comment that we knew what we purchased but not what we sold, that was an uncommon truth. Sales were not tracked by item, only by total dollars. Our vendors re-stocked the shelves in our stores and we relied on those reports as a good but not 100% reliable estimate of what was sold. The problem was solved when scanning was introduced in later years.

## Ratings, Opinions, and Other Assessment Techniques

Most audit departments now include some form of assessment, conclusion, or opinion in each of their audit reports.

A grading system is common, such as:

- Effective, satisfactory, or requires improvement. This is based on the assessed risk from the presence of control weaknesses

- Red, yellow, or green, where red indicates the presence of major deficiencies, yellow indicates there is a need for improvement, and green says that the controls are considered effective. Again, the grade is based on the level of risk posed by the identified deficiencies

Sometimes, there is no overall assessment per se. Instead, the report simply says whether there were 'major' or 'high risk' deficiencies, 'significant' or 'medium risk' issues, or only 'minor' issues (if any).

As a member of an internal audit department, this is what I was used to. When I became the leader of the internal audit function at Tosco, I started this way as well.

But I don't do that now.

In a risk-based audit approach, we are trying to provide assurance on whether the management of the risks that matter provides reasonable assurance that they will be at desired levels.

We are auditing the controls over the risks that matter so we can provide assurance on the management of those risks.

So we need to do more than say whether the controls are 'adequate' or that there are 'high' or 'major' risks.

We need to say whether the management of risks is adequate.

**And**..... we need to remember that these are *risks to enterprise objectives*.

We need to explain whether the achievement of any enterprise objectives is threatened (or, if you like, 'at risk') because of weaknesses in controls.

So, if we define the scope and objectives as addressing certain risks to objectives, the audit opinion should provide assurance on the management of those risks and objectives.

When we assess the significance of a control deficiency, it should be in this context. Does it indicate that the level of risk is outside desired levels?

The level of risk should <u>not</u>, in my opinion, be based on whether the potential effect is more than a certain value. It should be based on whether it is outside desired levels and therefore enterprise objectives may not be achieved.

I don't like grading systems.

I much prefer a method that answers one or both of two questions:

a.  Does this control deficiency, alone or in combination with others, mean that the level of risk is outside desired levels[72]?

---

[72] This is very similar to a 'material weakness' as defined for Sarbanes-Oxley compliance, or a 'major' deficiency as defined in the 2013 COSO *Internal Control – Integrated Framework* – see below.

b. Who, from operating management up to the CEO and the board, needs to take action? Who needs to own the corrective action and who needs to monitor the situation until that action has been completed?

I find that last one very useful. If a control deficiency or combination of deficiencies really is major or high risk, surely that means that a corporate objective will likely not be achieved – and that would merit the personal attention of the CEO and be monitored by the board.

If we want to say we are using a risk-based approach, we have to provide risk-based assurance. Is there reasonable assurance that risks are and will be at acceptable or desired levels?

If we don't provide that information, our professional opinion, I don't think we are doing our job[73].

### COSO Internal Control Framework and deficiencies

One of the nuggets in the 2013 update of COSO's *Internal Control – Integrated Framework* can be found in the 'Deficiencies in Internal Control' section. It says:

An internal control deficiency or combination of deficiencies that is severe enough to adversely affect the likelihood that the entity can achieve its objectives is referred to as a "major deficiency".

As I said above, deficiencies should not be assessed based on a defined value.

Deficiencies should be assessed based on whether they represent an unacceptable level of risk to one or more corporate objectives.

Earlier this year, I was asked by a senior audit executive of a large corporation to help her with a problem. Her audit had identified a control weakness that represented a potential loss to the organization of

---

[73] For some situations, where the area being audited is relatively immature, a maturity model may be a better alternative than a black-and-white assessment.

over a million dollars. She and her team had identified this as "high risk", but management believed that it was not. One of their arguments was that operating management could, and indeed had, resolve the issue fairly easily.

She was not satisfied and asked for my opinion.

I told her that I would not call it a "high risk" either.

Her face showed she was not satisfied, but I continued.

I pointed out that her company's revenue was more than $4 billion. While $1 million is a lot of money to her and to me, it was not to her company.

The opportunity to save $1 million did not merit the attention of the audit committee of the board. While they would find it interesting and congratulate the CAE, there was *nothing they needed to do* about it.

Similarly, the CEO would smile and say "well done" but do nothing more.

Even the CFO would quickly move on to issues that mattered to him.

I told her that since the issue had already been resolved to her satisfaction, no further action was required, and the issue did not require any senior executive to monitor or act on the information, I would not even include the issue in the final audit report!

It is difficult for internal auditors to understand that the issues they find may seem important, but are not necessarily so. This senior audit executive reluctantly accepted my view.

If we are to be perceived as performing audits that matter, providing assurance, insight, and advice that matters, we need to avoid communicating what does <u>not</u> matter.

If you were running the business, you need to know whether there is anything affecting your ability to achieve your objectives. Do you need to change or monitor anything?

If not, why are you wasting my time?

Commentary

The mission of internal audit is to provide assurance, advice, and insight[74].

Assurance is provided by our opinions, our professional assessment of whether the management of risk is adequate to provide reasonable assurance that objectives will be achieved.

In order to do that, we have to provide opinions that say whether the management of risk is adequate. Where there are deficiencies, we need to identify which risks may be outside desired levels and which enterprise objectives are 'at risk'.

Advice and insight is provided by our recommendations and other comments we communicate to management and the board – which I will cover in chapter 12.

---

[74] Based on the IIA's Mission and Principles for effective internal auditing.

## Chapter 10: How long is an audit?

The answer to this question[75] is "as long as you need to reach a conclusion about the risks being addressed."

Once that conclusion can be drawn, there is no need to keep auditing. All that remains is working with the management team to agree on any actions necessary and appropriate to improve operations, communicating the results of the engagement (discussed later), and finalizing necessary documentation.

At that point, the audit team will have completed and communicated its assessment (i.e., provided assurance), and agreed on action items (provided insight and advice).

Some people keep auditing when there is minimal added value in continuing. I had this experience at Home Savings of America[76].

> Home Savings was always updating and improving its computer systems and a major part of our work involved participating in major systems projects to ensure sufficient controls and security were included. The IT department and all the major business users supported internal audit involvement.
>
> One of my audit supervisors, an Assistant Vice President responsible for audits of the computer systems that supported the savings side of the business, was working on a major systems upgrade in the ATM banking area.
>
> Carla was an experienced IT auditor with excellent insight into the business side, having worked for a time in that area. To this day, I believe strongly in auditors who have line experience and therefore understand what it is like to run part of the business, especially when it includes responsibility for revenues and expenses.

---

[75] My Economics professor at the London School of Economics once told us that the correct answer to any question is "It depends".

[76] As told in *World Class Internal Auditing: Tales from my Journey*

Carla and I met to review the progress she had made. She explained that she had reviewed all the system deliverables to date, including the Requirements Definition, Systems Design, and draft User Procedures. Everything so far was looking good, but she was concerned that the project still had quite a long way to go and she had other projects that needed her attention.

We agreed that while it was desirable to continue to support this key project, our primary objective was to provide management with assurance that when it was implemented the controls over and security of the system and its data would be adequate.

Although the project team still had to complete development of the final product, test it, and turn it over to the users for their testing, the company's processes for testing and acceptance of the final product were excellent. Testing by IT and users was typically thorough, disciplined, and all we needed to do with regard to testing was to review the testing documentation once it was completed. The efficiency of the IT project was a minor element of our audit scope and given the other demands for Carla's attention, we should drop further related audit procedures.

In other words, we should see if we could assess whether the *design* of the system, its controls and security, would satisfy our criteria. If so, we could issue a preliminary report indicating that if the system was implemented *as designed*, our opinion was that the controls and security would be adequate. We could update that report when we had reviewed the testing documentation and confirmed that the controls, as designed, had been sufficiently tested and found to be operating as intended.

Carla was comfortable with this approach and we moved on to whether we had sufficient information with which to assess the design of the controls and security.

Carla thought she needed additional information and was planning to meet with several users and IT developers. I suggested we use a "control matrix" to help us see where we stood. A control matrix is a simple table where each column represents a type of system transaction, such as a deposit or withdrawal, and the rows are where you assess whether the controls satisfy defined control criteria. We used control criteria that were based on what I had learned at C&L: completeness, accuracy, validity, and maintenance. So you take each transaction, in turn, and assess whether the controls adequately ensure that all transactions are completely entered, processed, and recorded. The controls that address that requirement are documented in the 'completeness' row for that transaction, as well as the assessment that they are adequate. Then you move to the next row, the next criteria, and identify and assess the related controls.

We were able to complete the entire control matrix, filling in the controls that satisfied each control attribute for every transaction. As we got towards the end, Carla started showing signs of discomfort. By the time the matrix was full, she was visibly concerned. She acknowledged that all control criteria were satisfied for all major transactions. She also confirmed that she was confident in her understanding of the controls. But, her experience was telling her that more work was needed.

We revisited the objectives of the audit, namely to provide assurance that the controls and security of the system, when it was implemented, would be adequate. She agreed that the control matrix had asked all the necessary questions and that the controls we had identified met the company's needs. She was able to put her prior experience aside and recognize that we had sufficient information to stop work until the testing had been completed.

This was an interesting exercise for both of us. Sometimes it is difficult to know when to stop work. There is always more to do, especially when your audit customers like seeing you at their meetings, etc. The control matrix helped us make the right decision and stop when there was no real value to continuing. I have used other techniques at times, such as sitting down at the end of the day (you could do it at the beginning, but I prefer the end) and making a list of the information you need before you can provide your considered, professional opinion on the adequacy of the controls (or management or risk.

C. Northcote Parkinson wrote[77] that "work expands so as to fill the time available for its completion". Auditors can always find other risks and other opportunities for improvement if time permits.

But, even if the budget is for more hours, as soon as we can we should stop and move on to the next project.

I believe in 'stop and go auditing'.

The concept is that as soon as you can conclude that the risks that matter are being managed properly, stop. But, if you can see problems you should keep going – even if the budget will be exceeded.

Internal audit planning should be sufficiently agile to enable audits to be cut short or extended, based on the level of risk that is identified during the engagement.

### The ideal audit length

My rule of thumb is that audit should, with few exceptions, be 200 hours or less. An 80 hour audit is fine.

Why so short?

It fits in with my belief that internal audit must be agile and nimble.

If you think of an individual demonstrating agility, they generally take short steps.

When internal audit performs shorter engagements that focus on the few risks that matter, they are able to move quickly from audit to audit.

---

[77] *Parkinson's Law or the Pursuit of Progress* – a book I recommend without reservation.

I also believe that when audits are shorter, the staff will focus better on what matters and avoid being tempted to perform work or stray onto risks that don't really matter at the enterprise level.

If a board member, senior executive, or the CAE himself requests help or identifies an emerging risk that requires attention, it is much easier to get an audit going quickly if the staff are not tied up on massive audits.

But there are exceptions, including:

- Pre-implementation reviews of major new systems or other initiatives. I like internal audit to perform proactive consulting engagements that provide assurance that the security and controls will be sufficient to address significant risks related to major projects. These can take several months of work, although often not full time, and I am happy to budget the necessary hours

  Having said which, there may be opportunities to cut the work required by these reviews. For example, there are choices to be made in the scope of the review:

  - Should the scope include project management?

  - Should it include reviewing the Requirements Definition (or equivalent[78]) or start later, such as with the Detailed Design?

  - To what extent should the audit team be involved with testing? Should it rely on IT and user testing, review what has been done, or perform independent testing – and if so how much?

  - Are there any implementation or post-implementation activities meriting audit support?

  All of these decisions should be made based on the level of risk. In the story above, Carla and I agreed that we would rely on IT and user testing as there was a history of robust testing by both groups. There were no implementation or post-implementation issues where our involvement was justified (we had other projects

---

[78] I am using traditional systems development methodology terms here. Even if more modern approaches, such as Agile, are used the basic principles remain the same.

to work on) because our assessment of security and controls was that they would be effective if implemented as designed.

- Audits of major locations or business units that are the source of multiple enterprise risks. While I like to keep individual audits short and focused on a few risks that matter, sometimes a single location or unit may require a longer allocation of time to address multiple enterprise risks.

For example, at Solectron we had major manufacturing sites in locations such as Penang, Malaysia; Austin, Texas; Suzhou, China; and, Bordeaux, France. Each was the source of multiple risks that mattered to the enterprise, such as those relating to the sourcing of critical materials; financial reporting; manufacturing quality; information security; and more

The audit team had to travel to these locations, so it was in our interests to have them travel once. I sent a larger team than at other locations so we were able to keep the duration of the fieldwork to two weeks. In addition, management at these locations preferred that we perform one large audit instead of multiple small ones.

## Minimizing time in the field

Being prepared before starting work at the location is very important.

The traditional process involves performing another risk assessment at this point. The location of the business unit has been identified based on a risk-ranking of the audit universe, and the second risk assessment identifies the risks to the location or unit that should be included in the scope.

However, the *enterprise* risk assessment process described earlier has already identified which risks should be included in the scope – those enterprise risks where the source is at this location.

Even so, it is prudent to update the understanding of activities at the location, confirming that they have not changed. The agile audit department will be open to amending the scope of the audit, or even canceling it, if the contribution to the enterprise level risk by activities at this location has diminished.

I like to see the team get as much information about the location or unit they will visit before they start any fieldwork. Not only does this help them update the risk assessment, but the greater the understanding of the business, the greater their ability to understand what they see, assess the controls, and determine whether risks are being managed effectively.

Several years ago, I visited the audit team at Cisco Systems, Inc. Steve Berberich[79] led the IT audit group at that time and told me how the Cisco team ran analytics to understand business trends and other activity during their preparation for any audit. He explained that when introducing themselves to the manager of the area they would audit, instead of asking how the business was doing, they would ask questions about the reasons for the business trends.

This gave immediate credibility to the team in the eyes of management. It demonstrated an understanding and an interest in the business.

My experience is that when you arrive in the field armed with good insights into the business, the time you spend on the audit is both more efficient and more effective.

It is also true in my experience that disruption of the business is reduced when (a) the time in the field is minimized, and (b) the auditor knows what he or she is asking for.

In addition, the impact on the audit department budget is less when the time in the field is less. Hotels continue to increase in cost relative to other travel costs.

There have been times when I have been able to reduce time in the field to next to nothing.

For example, at Maxtor our regional HQ was in Singapore and that is where I had based my Asia Pacific team. We had a couple of factories in Singapore but our larger one was in Suzhou, China. Operations, business

---

[79] Steve is currently Director, GRC IT & Data Analytics Audit – Global at Cisco

processes, and the supporting computer systems were very much the same in Suzhou as in Singapore. All our locations operated off a single instance of the SAP ERP.

When it came time to perform controls testing (for SOX) in Suzhou, we decided that we could view all the transactions in the system from Singapore and ask that the accounting staff in Suzhou simply fax or email us the related documents. As a result, we were able to perform the testing without setting foot in Suzhou[80].

At Solectron, our approach at the smaller (and lower risk) sites was to rely where possible on management's answers to a self-assessment questionnaire. Sometimes, we needed more assurance that the controls were as they described, in which case we would ask them to email or fax supporting documents.

At an internal audit conference, a speaker who led the internal audit and SOX testing teams at his company told a similar story. They required control and process owners to answer a self-assessment questionnaire every quarter.

The speaker had added an interesting twist. Each quarter, management was required to provide a sample that showed the control in action (i.e., a copy of the documents involved). This provided a greater level of assurance that management had answered the questionnaire honestly and accurately. Sometimes, management answers based on what they believe or have directed rather than what they have determined on inspection of the process – what is actually happening.


How to staff the audit

Putting the best team on any audit is an art, not a science.

A number of factors go into the decision, including:

---

[80] We had previously performed walkthroughs and conducted similar testing in Suzhou.

- The skills and experience required. For example, do I need an IT auditor as well as an operational auditor? Do I need somebody with commodity trading experience as well as a financial auditor?

- The time available. Sometimes, there are constraints on the timing of the audit, such as the availability of management, the need to complete the audit before management is consumed by the period close, a commitment to another audit, the availability of audit staff (for example, vacations may be planned), and so on.

- The size of the audit. The more areas of risk to be addressed, the more likely I am to put more people on the audit.

- Limits on the time audit staff should be in the field. Like many others, I prefer to keep audits where the auditors have to travel to two weeks or less. This is better for team morale, enabling the team members to have a more balanced life. Complications may arise when people are away for an extended period, such as their desire to travel during weekends, who will pay for such trips, and so on.

- The location of the audit. My preference was to have my people close to the businesses they audited, so I had staff in several locations. While I would often mix up people from different locations (for example, to expose them to different ideas and experiences), more often the people closer to the location would be assigned audits at that location.

- The desire to train individuals. I will often try to pair new people to the team with auditors with more experience. The new auditors may also need to be assigned a variety of different types of engagements to help them learn the business.

- To add variety. While there are advantages to keeping people on the same type of audit, they may not enjoy that (with the risk that either people will leave or become stale) and their broader skills may not develop as needed for the longer term.

- Management preferences. More often than not in my experience, management likes to have shorter audits, even if that requires having more of the audit team on site.

In larger audit departments, the wishes of the engagement leader will come into play. They may prefer to work with smaller or larger teams. They may and often do have strong preferences as to who they like to work with. But, while I will listen to those requests, they do not override other issues, such as whether they are the best people for this particular engagement or whether they are more valuable on another audit.

## Commentary

Each CAE will typically have his or her own style when it comes to staffing. Perhaps they like to have semi-permanent teams, where the same group of auditors travel and audit together. Or, perhaps they prefer to have their auditors work in pairs or by themselves.

In an agile audit department, it is more likely that staffing will vary from audit to audit and that the size of the audit team on any engagement will be small.

But, it all depends on what is best – not just for a single engagement but for overall audit planning and the delivery of value to our stakeholders.

# Chapter 11: Audit documentation and working papers

Why do we spend our valuable and limited time on working papers? Answers I have heard include:

- Because we have always developed working papers? Maybe this is something learned while in public accounting

- So we can re-use the information in future audits

- Because the *Standards* require working papers

- Because the regulators, examiners, or others might audit our work

- So we can prove our point if challenged by management

- So we can demonstrate a quality program and pass the IIA Quality Assurance Review (QAR)

Each of these answers is common and merits our attention.

Good auditors would never accept as an answer to a question about why management does something, "Because that's the way we have always done it". Yet, many internal audit departments spend a fair amount of their time preparing working papers because they always have without ever questioning why.

My belief is that time should be spent documenting the work done **to the extent that it has value** greater than the cost.

I was initially trained at Coopers & Lybrand (now PwC) and learned a valuable lesson about the value – and cost – of working papers, even in a public accounting environment.

This is how I described it in *World-Class Internal Auditing: Tales from my Journey*.

> When I returned to the firm's offices at the end of the audit, I received a note from the group manager[81]. Gordon directed me

---

[81] In those days, a 'group manager' was responsible for thirty or more auditors and reported directly to the partners. Gordon Dow, mentioned here, as a very experienced manager and led one of the larger groups.

to take all the workpapers to the partner's office. The partner, Chris Lowe, wanted to review them. Now this was very unusual. Partners generally relied on the managers to review workpapers, but Gordon told me that Mr. Lowe wanted to see them. My guess was that he wanted to assure himself that all the work had been completed, because it was done so much faster than in the prior year.

I took them up to his office and left them with his secretary. Then I waited and waited, trying to be patient. I had confidence that all the work had been completed, but didn't feel good about the time the partner was taking to return them.

Eventually, I got them back with a note. Mr. Lowe wrote this:

"These are the best workpapers I have ever seen."

My heart leaped and a smile started to spread. But he continued:

"You spent too many hours on them."

Surprise!

My first reaction was confusion. I had completed the audit in record time and built nigh-on perfect workpapers in the process. Why was he complaining?

I asked Kevin[82]. He sat me down and congratulated me for the praise part of the note. Then he explained what Mr. Lowe was saying.

Kevin told me that every hour spent on an audit was a cost and as a partner Mr. Lowe saw any extra hours as reducing his personal share of the firm's profits. While the quality of my work was commendable, it didn't need to be that good.

Kevin explained that the good far outweighed the negative and that Mr. Lowe was actually very pleased with the audit.

---

[82] Kevin Gilbert was my manager.

However, the surprising criticism made a huge and lasting impression on me.

We must never forget that every hour spent on documentation has a cost: that hour could be spent on another audit engagement.

In years past, when we performed the same audit year after year, there was clear value. The description of the process and controls allowed us to avoid duplicating process documentation each year, and we would very often test the same controls in the same way each year.

But, today we have a dynamic, risk-based audit plan that has few audits that repeat the next year. It is true that an audit may come up again, a few years later, but by then it is highly likely that the business processes, systems, people, and more will have changed.

In fact, even if a process, location, or unit audit is audited again the next year, the scope (the enterprise risks being addressed) may be different. For example, I have often audited accounts payable a few years in a row – but the first was focused on the basic processes and controls, the second on payments to consultants and contractors, and the third on fraud risk.

In fact, repeating the same audit, using the prior year's audit program without questioning it, can lead to auditing the same controls in the same way when the risks have in fact changed.

In other words, the value of audit working papers to future audits is limited.

But don't the *Standards* require working papers? Will we pass the IIA QAR without extensive documentation of the work performed?

*Standard 2330* – Documenting Information says:

> Internal auditors must document relevant information to support the conclusions and engagement results.

This is thin, but Practice Advisory 2330-1, *Documenting Information*[83], provides further guidance:

---

[83] The Practice Advisory is considered 'recommended guidance' and was published in 2009.

1. Internal auditors prepare working papers. Working papers document the information obtained, the analyses made, and the support for the conclusions and engagement results. Internal audit management reviews the prepared working papers.

2. Engagement working papers generally:

   - Aid in the planning, performance, and review of engagements.

   - Provide the principal support for engagement results.

   - Document whether engagement objectives were achieved.

   - Support the accuracy and completeness of the work performed.

   - Provide a basis for the internal audit activity's quality assurance and improvement program.

   - Facilitate third-party reviews.

3. The organization, design, and content of engagement working papers depend on the engagement's nature and objectives and the organization's needs. Engagement working papers document all aspects of the engagement process from planning to communicating results. The internal audit activity determines the media used to document and store working papers.

4. The chief audit executive establishes working paper policies for the various types of engagements performed. Standardized engagement working papers, such as questionnaires and audit programs, may improve the engagement's efficiency and facilitate the delegation of engagement work. Engagement working papers may be categorized as permanent or carry-forward engagement files that contain information of continuing importance.

The key is interpreting point 3 in this recommended, but not mandatory guidance.

"The organization, design, and content of engagement working papers depend on the engagement's nature and objectives and the organization's needs."

I interpret this as saying that the investment in working papers should be commensurate with the value they represent.

With respect to the remaining reasons mentioned at the start of this chapter, working papers may be of value in the following situations.

- Where internal audit work is relied upon by others, such as the external auditor, or will be reviewed by regulators or examiners[84].

  At Tosco, my team performed required annual audits of the company's compliance with Foreign Trade Zone regulations. Our work was audited every year by examiners from a federal government agency[85]. I was proud that the quality of the working papers was pronounced each year as the best they had seen.

- When the results of the engagement may be the subject of litigation, disciplinary actions based at least in part on the audit work, or similar. The working papers should be able to stand up to the scrutiny of opposing counsel and the court.

- It is always possible that management might challenge our assessment of the condition of controls and the management of risk. If it is necessary to go back to the working papers to produce evidence regarding the facts underlying the assessment, then there is value. But.....

---

[84] Many regulated industries have this situation. However, there has to be more than just the *potential* for a third party examiner or auditor to review internal audit work. For example, I spoke at an IIA chapter in Southern California to a group where most of the people worked for local government agencies. They said they did working papers and spent a lot of time making sure they were of very high quality, because state auditors might audit them. When I asked when the state had last audited, none of them could recall a visit from the state auditors in the last 20 years.

[85] In 2016, the agency that performs the audits is US Customs and Border Protection, an agency within the US Department of Homeland Security.

- ○ If the audit team communicated their findings, as they should, during the fieldwork rather than waiting to discuss the report, then the facts should already be agreed with management.

- ○ Disagreement on the facts is, in my experience, unusual. It is far more common to disagree on the interpretation of those facts – the significance of any control deficiency (the level of risk they represent), whether corrective action should be taken to reduce the risk, and what that action should be. I am not persuaded that the working papers add value to that discussion.

- ○ Typical working papers cover far more than the detail needed to support internal audit's position when management disagrees.

- Working papers enable a review of the work performed by the CAE or other internal audit manager. As explained in the Practice Advisory, leadership of the internal audit function needs to ensure that each engagement was of the desired quality and the assessment is fair and balanced. But, how detailed and comprehensive should the working papers be to support that requirement?

### How to review the work of the audit staff

Working papers can be an aid in reviewing the work of the staff, but we need to remember our objectives in so doing:

1. To obtain assurance that the work was completed as required and that the results of the engagement (the assessment and any advice and insights) are valid, fair, and balanced; and,

2. To help audit management assess and contribute to the improved performance of the engagement audit team.

The working papers will generally provide the reviewer with evidence that the work has been done and the audit program completed.

But, does it provide sufficient evidence that *quality* work was done and that the assessment, advice, and insight in the audit report provide management with the information they need?

When the audit involves support for the external auditor, is likely to be reviewed by an examiner or similar, or may be subpoenaed in litigation, I will always ensure a careful review is performed.

But, for most audit engagements, the working papers are incidental for me.

I prefer instead to have a conversation with the lead auditor (and other members of the team as necessary) to ensure I am satisfied that sufficient work was performed, the assessment and findings can be supported, and that I agree with and can support that assessment.

A conversation enables more to be brought out than will ever be in the working papers. It is especially useful in ensuring that the root cause of any issues has been properly identified and that all valuable insights and advice will be shared with management.

A conversation is also an opportunity to mentor the audit team lead and to improve my own understanding of the business. When we talk about the business, that discussion will generally help both of us. I can share my broader perspective and he or she can share the reality on the ground.

I especially like to learn as much as I can about the strength of the people in the area audited, both in management and at a staff level, and their morale. There may be a larger issue, such as the culture of the organization, or the quality of leadership and management.

When I listen to the audit staff in these situations, I can improve my own understanding of their potential, opportunities for improvement, and obtain feedback on the audit department as a whole and its management – including my own management.

Every discussion is an opportunity for mentoring and providing feedback, especially as more and more organizations move away from formal staff appraisals.

Commentary

Internal auditing has value but it also has a cost.

We need to ensure that every internal audit hour, every dollar, is spent wisely.

Following Lean methodology, we need to ensure that every hour is spent on something that creates or is necessary in support of the valuable service we provide to the organization.

Working papers have traditionally consumed a great deal of time.

I am not saying that we should dispense with them.

I am saying that we should challenge the time we spend on them, investing in their preparation consistent with the value they represent.

In other words, don't develop working papers because that is what we have always done. Do them because they are necessary and valuable.

# Chapter 12: Communicating the results of the audit engagement

Most internal auditors do not realize that the *Standards* do not require that every audit conclude with a formal, written, audit report.

The *Standards* only require that the results of the engagement be *communicated*. They do not specify that the communication has to be in a formal, written report.

Here are the most relevant Standards:

### 2400 – Communicating Results

Internal auditors must communicate the results of engagements.

### *2410 – Criteria for Communicating*

Communications must include the engagement's objectives and scope as well as applicable conclusions, recommendations, and action plans.

> **2410.A1** - Final communication of engagement results must, where appropriate, contain the internal auditors' opinion and/or conclusions. When issued, an opinion or conclusion must take account of the expectations of senior management, the board, and other stakeholders and must be supported by sufficient, reliable, relevant, and useful information.
>
> **Interpretation:**
> *Opinions at the engagement level may be ratings, conclusions, or other descriptions of the results. Such an engagement may be in relation to controls around a specific process, risk, or business unit. The formulation of such opinions requires consideration of the engagement results and their significance.*
>
> **2410.A2** – Internal auditors are encouraged to acknowledge satisfactory performance in engagement communications.

**2410.C1**[86] – Communication of the progress and results of consulting engagements will vary in form and content depending upon the nature of the engagement and the needs of the client.

### 2420 – Quality of Communications

Communications must be accurate, objective, clear, concise, constructive, complete, and timely.

Interpretation:

*Accurate communications are free from errors and distortions and are faithful to the underlying facts. Objective communications are fair, impartial, and unbiased and are the result of a fair-minded and balanced assessment of all relevant facts and circumstances. Clear communications are easily understood and logical, avoiding unnecessary technical language and providing all significant and relevant information. Concise communications are to the point and avoid unnecessary elaboration, superfluous detail, redundancy, and wordiness. Constructive communications are helpful to the engagement client and the organization and lead to improvements where needed. Complete communications lack nothing that is essential to the target audience and include all significant and relevant information and observations to support recommendations and conclusions. Timely communications are opportune and expedient, depending on the significance of the issue, allowing management to take appropriate corrective action.*

Communicating results to stakeholders

It is critical not only to *audit* what matters, but to *communicate* what matters.

---

[86] The Standard also includes 2410.A3 – When releasing engagement results to parties outside the organization, the communication must include limitations on distribution and use of the results.

211

It is not about communicating what matters to the auditor.

It is about communicating what matters to each of our stakeholders – in operating management, senior and executive management, on the board, and others as appropriate (e.g., regulators and external auditors).

Operating management need to know when anything beyond the trivial is not working the way they intend.

I expect the audit team to communicate that information, relevant insights about root causes and so on, and actionable advice about how to correct the situation as soon as possible.

Let me emphasize that last phrase: "as soon as possible".

Why delay correction of a deficiency? The risk continues until addressed, so I always want at least an informal discussion promptly with management to give them the opportunity to take action to bring the risk within acceptable limits.

If it makes sense to have a control because of the risk, it makes sense to correct it and the internal auditor must enable that correction by providing appropriate information in a timely fashion.

The auditor doesn't have to wait for the closing meeting, let alone the audit report, to share information with appropriate management. While external auditors may be afraid[87] of sharing information before the 'finding' has been reviewed with the senior, manager, and partner, that should never be the case with internal auditors.

Our goal is not to find fault[88]. It is to help management improve their processes, where necessary, through our advice and insight.

---

[87] I fully understand the external auditors' concern about the risk to their firm should they communicate information that is incorrect. They want information (such as the detection of control deficiencies) and the communication of it to be approved by at least a manager. However, that can be a client-service problem if a significant issue is not communicated promptly to management and the potential for fraud or other risk remains unaddressed for an unacceptable period of time.

[88] The value and quality of internal audit work should **never** be judged on the basis of how many issues they find.

If management responds with alacrity to correct issues, then this should be recognized in the final audit report[89].

If there is no value in informing more senior management that there was an issue, then I typically won't mention it – except, perhaps, to say that "additional issues were identified during the audit that were immediately corrected by management". If I do mention it because the risk, until corrected, was significant, I will also indicate that the risk has now been addressed by management.

There is no harm, and every good, in commending management for their commitment to controls. Apart from complying with Standard 2410.A2 ("Internal auditors are encouraged to acknowledge satisfactory performance in engagement communications"), it helps build a solid relationship with management. In addition, the fact that operating management has shown this commitment should be reassuring to executive management and the board.

A Closing Meeting is held at the end of every audit. This is an opportunity to review the results of the engagement with management before leaving the field. Many if not most audit departments share a draft of the full audit report at that meeting, although I prefer only to share the detailed findings. I prefer to wait until after the Closing Meeting to share a complete draft so I can:

(a) Obtain feedback from management on the issues and our preliminary assessment, and

(b) Consider how best to frame the assessment in our communication

Although the issues we identified during the audit have typically been discussed with direct management (those directly responsible for the control), the Closing Meeting is usually attended by department heads and other more senior management. They may not have been informed about all of the issues and this is an opportunity for the audit team to

---

[89] Consistent with Standard 2410.A2.

explain what they found, why it is important, confirm the facts, and agree on whether corrective action is needed.

Each of these is very important.

Management needs to know and understand what we found before they can be expected to agree on the facts and their interpretation – does this represent a risk of significance, what action is required, by whom, and when.

There is no excuse, in my opinion, for failing to confirm the facts at the Closing Meeting and then having a dispute when the draft audit report is shared with management.

Equally, the audit team needs to listen to the management team and their assessment of the risk represented by any deficiency. Disagreements after the report has been drafted are a waste of everybody's time and do little for the audit department's reputation.

Very often, the corrective action is agreed and even assigned in the Closing Meeting.

Executive management[90] doesn't need all the details; they should be able to rely on their direct reports in operating management to take care of them.

I like to ask the question: "What do they need to know?" They need to know anything that:

- They need to act on;

- They need to monitor; or,

- Represents a significant and unacceptable risk to their or the organization's objectives.

Anything beyond that is not just immaterial to them, but can actually degrade the quality of the report.

---

[90] What constitutes 'executive management' will vary from organization to organization. I tend to include the people to whom the most senior person in the Closing Meeting reports all the way up to the CEO.

As an aside (which is why this section is indented), I learned the hard way not to include in the audit report issues that executive management don't need to know – issues that can be handled at a lower level.

As a young IT audit manager with Coopers & Lybrand in Los Angeles[91], I led a special project commissioned by the CFO of the Golden Nugget (which at that time operated two casinos, one in Las Vegas and one in Atlantic City). The engagement was to audit the controls over all the financial back-office systems supporting the Las Vegas operation.

Let's just say that the controls were pervasively weak. I can remember that the calculation of depreciation in the fixed assets system continued even after an asset's net book value was zero. We found multiple assets where depreciation was still being calculated even though net book value was negative.

Our audit report ran close to 100 pages because the firm's standard format required that every finding or group of findings started on a new page.

While there was a two page executive summary, I was still mildly concerned about what the CFO's reaction would be when he saw the draft report.

I should have been more than mildly concerned!

The CFO was furious!

He confronted me. He asked whether I was trying to make him look bad, as the final report would be shared with the CEO and then with the audit committee of the board. Somewhat timidly, I asked whether any of the issues were either factually incorrect or unfairly presented. He replied that they were factually correct and what we said about them was accurate.

---

[91] I was young in experience if not in age.

But, the impression created by the report as a whole was unjustified, in his opinion. Clearly, he regretted hiring us (and me in particular).

We did what we could, including taking out issues that were minor and didn't merit executive attention.

I don't think his outrage was without justification.

As internal auditors, we have to consider **why** we are communicating the results of our engagement.

We communicate the information that our stakeholders need to perform their oversight and leadership roles.

We don't communicate to make ourselves look good, to prove our value.

We simply cannot afford to create the impression that we are out to find fault and prove our value at management's expense.

Our job is to help management and the board succeed.

We need to make it easy for busy executives to read, absorb, and then act on the results of our work.

I covered this topic in *World-Class Internal Auditing: Tales from my Journey*. In the following excerpt, I discuss how I decided on audit report design as the new head of internal audit at Tosco Corporation by reflecting on lessons learned at previous companies.

> Mario Antoci, the President of [Home Savings of America], received a copy of our internal audit reports. He tasked his executive secretary with reading every report and highlighting the sections he needed to read. If there was nothing meriting his attention in the report, it was filed. If there were items of significance, she brought that to his attention straight away.
>
> My initial thought [at Tosco] was that I would highlight the audit reports for the board and top executives. But then I asked myself why the audit report had sections that they didn't need to read.
>
> I talked to my key stakeholders in management and on the audit committee and listened carefully so I could understand what they needed to hear after an audit was completed.

I heard them say that they wanted to know the answers to two questions:

1. Is there anything they need to worry about?

2. Are there any issues of such significance that somebody in senior management should be monitoring how and when they are addressed?

In other words, they wanted to manage by exception. They were going to trust internal audit and operating management to address routine issues; they didn't want to waste their time (my expression; they didn't actually use those words) on matters that didn't merit their attention.

So, I designed a cover sheet for every audit report. It was simple and to the point. It looked like this.

---

January 15, 1995

Audit of Derivatives Trading

- Are there any risk issues of significance to the Audit Committee or executive management? YES/**NO**
- Are there any outstanding major internal control findings meriting Audit Committee or executive management attention? YES/**NO**

<u>Distribution:</u>
Audit Committee
Executive and Operating Management

---

If either of the answers to the two questions on the cover page was "Yes", I would include a sentence (at most two) explaining the issue. Then they could read the rest of the report (or at least the Executive Summary) for more.

If the answers were both "No", unless they had a particular interest in the topic addressed by the audit, they might not read further – and they didn't need to.

The cover sheet worked exceptionally well. Executives could read, pretty much at a glance, whether there was something serious that merited their immediate attention.

In my experience, even with a one-page audit report most executives will delay reading it until after they have 'reading time'. Sometimes that may mean that the report is not read until the weekend.

I continued to describe my approach in the book.

All of these people are severely limited in the amount of time they can devote to reading audit reports, so it was up to me to ensure I communicated what they needed to know in a way that they could read and understand it quickly.

The cover sheet was the first part of my answer to that question.

There was more that I wanted to do to make sure my audit reports were easy for board members and executives.

I wanted to avoid the need for anybody, including myself, to have to highlight what the executives and board members needed to read.

I wanted the audit report to be the highlighted content, with everything else either omitted or relegated either to the end of the report, included as an attachment, communicated in another way (e.g., to operating management at the closing meeting), or omitted entirely.

In other words, I wanted the executives to be able to read just the first few paragraphs and obtain the most critical information and satisfy their needs.

The first page of the audit report, behind the cover page, is an Executive Summary and starts with the most important piece of information the executives needed to hear: our opinion on the adequacy of the controls over the risks included in our scope.

[The following] is the first part of the Executive Summary of a report from my team at Business Objects.

---

Executive Summary

In our opinion, adequate controls exist to ensure that the required level of approval is obtained when discounting license deals.

However, there is no analysis detailing the discounts granted by deal, product, country, sales channel, etc. Without this discount reporting, it is nearly impossible to measure the financial impact of discounting on the Company or the effectiveness of our discounting strategy. A global discount report is being created detailing discounts granted by country, region, territory, sales rep, PLU for direct sales (Mid-Market and Enterprise) in both EMEA and Americas. The plan is to test and deploy the report in Q1 2008 and roll out to sales management in EMEA and Americas.

---

I said earlier that I believe internal audit should provide an opinion: their assessment of the condition of controls and whether they provide assurance that the risks in scope are managed at desired levels.

I like, whenever possible, for the reader of the audit report to see that immediately.

It's the most important piece of information we communicate, so it should be front and center.

The only exception is where it is necessary to provide some context before the reader will understand our assessment – what it covers, why it should be important to them, and so on.

After the opinion, we answer the question "are there any issues of significance" and "do they require my attention".

I am not easily persuaded that anything else needs to be in the audit report.

If there are facts or issues that don't require an executive's attention, why do we need to tell him or her about them?

The executive is entitled to place reliance on operating management to address less significant issues – issues that we communicated in the Closing Meeting.

So, every item that the audit team wants to include in the report that goes beyond what I can see an executive needing to know will come into question from me.

## Findings and recommendations

Internal audit provides assurance, advice, and insights. According to the IIA, the mission of internal audit is:

> "To enhance and protect organizational value by providing risk-based and objective assurance, advice, and insight."

The opinion or assessment provides the *assurance* our stakeholders need in running the business.

The 'findings and recommendations' provide *advice and insight*.

I believe it is very important for internal auditors, especially the CAE, to understand that the word 'finding' can have negative connotations. It can sound like 'gotcha' to management, especially if there are financial or other repercussions for a manager should an audit identify control deficiencies.

One of the challenges I faced at Solectron was that senior management responsible for our Asia-Pacific/Japan operations believed that the managers responsible for each operation should have their bonus cut if internal audit reported control deficiencies.

When I found out, I appealed to the senior executive responsible for that policy to change it. I argued that while it showed a commendable commitment to internal control and the management of risk, the better approach (in my opinion) was for only major or significant risk and control issues to affect their performance evaluation.

Unfortunately, that appeal fell on deaf ears.

The effect of this policy was that management fought internal audit tooth and nail:

- They would battle not to have their operation included in the audit plan. They would say that their activity was the highest performing and best-run in the company. We should audit the poor-performing areas.

  While we always listened, we remained true to our risk-based audit approach; while their operation probably was well-run, it was also the largest and certainly a major source of risk if controls were not operating effectively.

- Once we told them their operation would be on our audit plan, they would perform their own audit to make sure everything was working well. Perhaps half of one of their finance manager's time was spent performing audits ahead of an internal audit[92]. This was not a good use of company funds. It would have been better if each process and control owner always, not just in advance of an audit, monitored important controls to ensure they were as desired.

  They were less concerned with managing risk to the operation and more concerned with managing risk to their individual compensation.

- If we found a control deficiency, whether in design or in operation, they would battle us on every front. Earlier, I told the story about how Wendy Ng found a serious segregation of duties problem. Management fought this all the way, even to the point where their CIO for Asia-Pacific tried to tell me that they had a compensating control – they didn't inform people what access rights they had.

I don't consider the audit report to be our final product.

---

[92] The individual was both a trained accountant and a certified internal auditor (CIA). But even though he would perform what might be a quality audit (we never saw it), our internal audit team still found control weaknesses.

Change is our final product.

A finding and recommendation has no value unless it leads to a necessary and appropriate change by management.

The last but certainly not least important of the IIA's twelve Core Principles for the Professional Practice of Internal Auditing is:

"Promotes positive change"

We must make every reasonable effort to communicate in a fashion that is not judgmental, is fair and balanced, will not be perceived as 'gotcha' auditing, and will influence appropriate and necessary change.

In some organizations, the word 'finding' is accepted and is not considered a problem for management. Others are different. Perhaps the word 'issue' will be accepted more readily as part of a constructive conversation.

I make sure I understand the situation and my team tries to use language that is clear, fair, balanced, concise, and constructive.

Some have developed rules for writing findings. For example, the rules might require the auditor to follow a specific format and describe the desired state, what they found, why there is a control deficiency, and the risk it represents.

I don't have such rules about format.

The only rule I have is that the auditor communicate in a way that both informs management of what they need to know and promotes positive change.

Rather than dictate wording or even format, I allow the auditor to structure the report in the way he or she believes will be more effective as a communication vehicle.

I tell my team that the English language is a rich one and that they should endeavor to make full use of it to communicate clearly their assessment, advice, and insight.

There are important subtleties in how we work with management and describe in the report the change that should be made.

The traditional approach is for internal audit to write the finding and a recommendation. Then they ask management to write a response. So, for each finding there is an explanation of the issue by internal audit, a recommendation by internal audit, and a management response. That response may include commentary on the issue and its severity by management as well as a description of the corrective action, if any, they will take.

In most cases, the recommendation and the management response are aligned. But, sometimes there is a difference of opinion.

A report where there is a difference of opinion between internal audit and management is a 'lose-lose-lose' situation.

Internal audit loses because they appear:

    a.   at odds with management;

    b.   unable to agree with management on the assessment and the appropriate and necessary corrective actions that should be taken; and

    c.   to have either failed to understand the business and its operating constraints or to explain to management why the issue is significant and requires correction.

Management loses because the audit committee will question their:

- commitment to controls and the management of risk;
- inability to 'educate' internal audit in the business and its operating realities;
- cooperation with the audit team; and,
- inability to resolve disagreement before it comes to the audit committee.

The audit committee loses because:

    a.   they are not sure whom to believe;

b. they do not receive the assurance they need to fulfil their oversight responsibilities and have to be the judge between audit and management;

c. their confidence in internal audit effectiveness wilts when the CAE seems unable to work with management; and,

d. their confidence in senior management wanes when they are unable to work effectively with internal audit.

These days, the great majority of internal audit functions work hard to avoid disagreements with management. While they retain their control and ownership of the audit assessment or opinion, they make every effort to listen to management to understand their perspective. Where disagreement remains, they work equally hard to explain their point of view.

People may disagree. That is real life.

But, when it comes to serious issues, all sides should be able to come together.

If the issues are not serious, perhaps they can be handled without the need to display disagreements in front of top management or the audit committee. In fact, they may not rise to the level where they need either party's attention and can be omitted from the audit report.

I don't like the appearance of the format that includes a finding, recommendation, and response.

As a rule, the recommendation and response should be the same – so there is little value in repeating the same information in different words.

I prefer to communicate the issue and then the *agreed action items*.

If we agree on the actions to be taken, then why disguise them as recommendations and responses.

Let's call them what they are: 'agreed action items'.

This sends a clear message that internal audit and management are working together to define and then solve any problem.

The audit committee wants to see this almost as much as they want to understand whether there are any serious issues.

They need to have confidence in both internal audit and the management team.

They want to see a commitment from management to controls and the management of risk, and that internal audit and management are working effectively together to resolve problems and effect positive change.

The agreed action items will show:

- What will be done

- By whom

- When

As I look back on the audit reports my team wrote at Tosco, Solectron, Maxtor, and Business Objects, there are similarities and differences.

- The executive or board member reading any report will quickly be able to see and understand our assessment. They don't have to search for it. In fact, it is generally in the first sentence of the first paragraph of the report[93].

- They focus on the significant and the immaterial is either omitted or relegated to an attachment.

- Context, such as a background section, is unusual. It is only provided when necessary to understand the situation and its significance to the business.

- We never talk about sample sizes or other details of the audit methodology. The reader simply doesn't need to know.

- The reports are short. Executive summaries are two pages at most, usually a single page.

However, the style once you move beyond the assessment to our advice and insight varies significantly. It is designed not only to communicate

---

[93] One CAE has told me that he put the assessment in bold in the second paragraph. That would also work well.

what the reader needs to know, but also to demonstrate the ability of audit and management to work towards our common goal of efficient and effective controls to manage risk, and to help management when it comes to taking the agreed corrective actions.

## Moving to modern communication methods

We need to remember that the task is not to write an audit report. It is to *communicate*.

We need to communicate in a way that is easy for the individual with whom we desire to communicate to receive, absorb, and act on the information they need from us.

Every CAE should take full advantage of modern communication methods – as well as taking more advantage of the oldest way to communicate (which I will discuss in a moment).

These days, executives receive the majority of their information in dashboards and similar forms, as well as in meetings and emails.

I believe the world-class CAE will understand how each of his key partners in management and on the board like to receive information, especially the information they want to get from internal audit.

I see nothing wrong with the CAE asking that the CEO's and CFO's daily dashboard or metrics include a section that highlights audit-related issues meriting that executive's attention.

Sometimes, that is enough.

If the executive needs to know that the audit engagement confirmed that controls over a specified risk are working effectively, then that can be communicated with a descriptor and a green light.

If controls were not adequate and the CEO's or CFO's attention is necessary, a red light replaces the green one, and a link is provided to the detail (which may be the audit report in full or abbreviated form).

This technique, when allied to the use of the oldest communication tool, can be effective. It gets the busy executive the information they need promptly, in a way that is easily consumed.

The oldest communication tool is *talking*.

When a simple "everything is OK" is insufficient, I believe the audit report is only the *start* of the communication.

A face-to-face discussion where the auditor can explain what he or she found, the implications, as well as share his or her advice and insight is invaluable.

A meeting provides the executive with the opportunity to ask questions and make sure he or she fully understands the situation before making decisions and taking actions.

The auditor needs to be disciplined in these meetings, making sure that he or she is *listening* actively to the executive.

As I mentioned earlier, it is critical to understand the root cause of any risk or control issue – and very often the root cause relates to people.

Talking about people problems is a challenge. It is an almost impossible problem in writing, for many reasons that include potential litigation. However, a careful discussion is an opportunity that should be seized in these tough situations.

At Tosco, I had two of these situations that may illustrate the point.

The first was during an audit of the commercial accounting activity at Tosco's refining division. A serious billing error (in the billions, no less) was the result of a combination of control failures. The root cause was the inability of the manager of the area to delegate. He kept all decisions and reviews to himself and gave his staff only clerical tasks. As a result, he worked an average of 12 hours each day and was unable to perform important tasks with consistent quality. His lack of trust and confidence in his people created a high risk of continued control failures.

The risk to the company was high. While I was able to include a reference to the problem in the report (written with care and the support of Human Resources), the real communication came in one-on-one discussions with senior management. The discussion ensured management had all the facts upon which to make an informed and appropriate decision; corrective action was quick and appropriate.

I described the second situation in *World-Class Internal Audit: Tales from my Journey*. Loretta Forti is our heroine, conducting an audit that focused on the timeliness of approval for capital expenditures (Authorizations for Expenditures, or AFEs). Here are relevant excerpts:

> It was relatively easy to find out how the process worked. Once a month, the division CFO gathered all the Vice Presidents and they collectively reviewed all the AFEs and the analysis prepared by Mike Passaretti and his team [the Capital Expenditure department]. They would take about half a day to discuss them and decide which they would propose should move forward and what the priority was for each.

> The next meeting, typically the following day, was with the division CEO, Bob. The CFO and all the Vice Presidents would review with Bob the AFEs they believed should go forward. When he felt that the total was too high or disagreed with the VPs' recommendations, the executives had to debate which would be approved, which might be deferred, and which would be declined. This meeting also took a half-day on average.

> Because of the intense review and approval process, each executive was careful to ensure all the AFEs they proposed had complete and accurate analyses included in the package. Mike and his team were equally careful with their review and analysis. This all took time.

> It was clear to Loretta, as it was to all the Vice Presidents and the CFO, that the process was too long, consumed far too much executive time, and often cost more than the spending itself (if you count the cost of the VPs' time)!

> The question was why the process was this way.

> The CFO and VPs all agreed, usually with language they wouldn't use with children around, that they hated both the all-VP meeting and the meeting with Bob. They said they didn't have the time to spare and asked for our help to get the process – both time and cost – under control.

Loretta and I met to talk about what we were to do. Rather than share my opinion, for once I did the smart thing and asked Loretta for her opinion.

At first, she didn't know what to say. But as she realized she could say what was on her mind, and with some gentle guidance from me, she said it: the CEO was the problem. He was the only one who wanted these long and expensive meetings. Only when he was persuaded to change his mind could it be changed.

I knew Bob quite well, having worked with him before he moved into his current position with the company. He was one of the executives with whom I met frequently to discuss the business and he had shared a number of confidences with me.

I was sure that he would listen to Loretta and had a suspicion he would find it easier to understand himself if he met one-on-one with her. Both a formal meeting with the CFO present and a larger meeting with the three of us (Bob, Loretta, and I) might make it harder for him to look in the mirror.

And so it was. I persuaded him to meet with Loretta and she, in turn, trusted me when I told her she would not only be safe but would enjoy herself.

I admit that I was a little nervous as I waited in my office for Loretta. Then she appeared in the doorway, all smiles!

She told me that the meeting went brilliantly. Bob was charming, as usual, and showed great respect for her – even though she was 'only' a manager. He let her explain what she had found and that the long process was preventing timely investment to seize market opportunities. In addition, not only was it consuming a lot of expensive executive time, but it was taking them away from running the business.

This was critical, explaining the issue in terms of how it affected the business and its success. Auditors who talk in their language (what I call "technobabble"), rather than the language of the executives they are attempting to inform or persuade (which is the objective of an audit report) are unlikely to succeed.

Loretta said that Bob responded with silence, clearly thinking about what she had said.

Then he shocked her by telling her that he was the problem. He recognized that his insistence on discussing and approving every AFE could not continue. Bob told Loretta she had done an excellent job and that he would like to talk to me.

When I met Bob later that week, he repeated his praise for Loretta. Then he asked for my opinion. Again I was smart and didn't give him my opinion straight away. Instead, I asked him why he wanted to approve every AFE.

After a short hesitation, he said that perhaps he should only approve major capital expenditures instead of every one. I concurred, saying that was what I was used to and would advise.

But I kept at it. Why had he insisted on approving every AFE? This was not what he had done in his previous positions with the company, nor was it what he was used to working directly for Tom O'Malley – a consistent and effective delegator.

Then he looked again in the mirror and saw his true self.

"Norman, I can see now that I didn't trust my direct reports enough to make these decisions!"

We talked about this for a while. Either he had the wrong people in these key positions, in which case he needed to replace them, or he needed to trust the people he had and delegate more effectively. He didn't hesitate before saying he had excellent people; he just had to let go, take a little more risk, and trust and delegate.

For the next couple of weeks, Loretta and I had a trail of VPs visiting us to express their thanks for Loretta's great work. Bob had changed the entire process, with new delegations of authority such that the VPs could approve most AFEs, the CFO would have to approve all over a certain value, and Bob was only involved in truly major capital expenditures.

In addition to these meetings with executives, called for the specific purpose of discussing the results of an audit, I met regularly with each of the key executives in the business.

I can't say that I met with every executive on a regular basis. While that would have been ideal, I simply didn't have the luxury of that amount of time.

Instead, I made it a point to meet with the executives responsible for the areas and risks with which I was most concerned.

### Communicating with the Audit Committee

The audit committees that I worked for all elected to receive a copy of every audit report. Even at Tosco, where we might produce 200 audit reports in a year, each member of the audit committee wanted to have the opportunity to see the results of each audit engagement promptly[94].

This was relatively easy with the cover page I described above, as they could see at a glance whether any audit had identified issues that needed their attention.

But that's not always the case. Many audit committees prefer to receive only a summary of the results of audits at their periodic meetings.

However, they should still be notified promptly should serious issues be identified between meetings.

With each audit committee, and whenever there was a change in the chair of that committee, I would initiate a discussion of what they wanted to see, when, and how.

The chair and I would agree on the conditions for a call (they all preferred that to an email) between meetings. Our agreement would then be ratified by the full committee.

---

[94] Only to be expected when each audit addressed risks that mattered to the enterprise.

Typically, we would agree that I should call him or her should we identify a serious internal control failure (and we would define what that meant), a fraud in excess of a certain value, or an important issue potentially involving a senior member of management.

The chair always emphasized that I was to discuss the issue with the CFO and, if necessary, the CEO before calling – unless, in my opinion, the situation demanded a confidential call. For example, if a senior executive might be involved, neither of us wanted that executive to be alerted.

Fortunately, I only had to make this kind of call a few times.

More frequent were the 'normal' calls or visits that I had with the audit committee chair and members.

Building and then maintaining a trusted relationship with the audit committee is essential.

Each member, not just the chair, needs to have confidence in the integrity, objectivity, competence, judgment, and fairness of the CAE. That confidence should extend to at least the CAE's direct reports.

In addition to periodic calls and meetings with the chair and each of the members, they would meet with each of my direct reports at least once a year (sometimes with the full audit department). This was an opportunity for my team to hear from the audit committee chair (and they appreciated not only the level of interest, the voter of confidence, the sharing of insights about the organization and its objectives, but the desire of the chair to get to know them).

The meetings with my direct reports were never very long; they might last an hour, but were usually shorter.

But, the meetings and calls I held with the chair and members were longer.

When a new director joined the audit committee (sometimes, I would meet with new directors who were not on the audit committee), he or she would first receive a level of orientation from management and the chair of the audit committee. He or she would then meet with me, generally in person and one-on-one, so I could share such matters as:

- The general condition of the systems of internal control and risk management

- Whether there were specific issues of significance that remained open or for other reasons should be brought to the new director's attention

- The charter, mission, and general approach of the internal audit department

- My comments on relationships with management and the external auditor

- Any concerns I might have on other areas, such as the control environment[95] or the ability of the information systems to support the organization and its goals

I had a new director orientation package (it might include a copy of the charters of the audit committee and internal audit department; copies of audit reports; our last audit plan; and so on) that I would prepare in consultation with the chair of the audit committee.

The orientation meeting was an excellent opportunity to start building the relationship with the new director that both of us desired. I would get to know his or her major concerns and interests, and he or she would gain insight into my background, competence, experience, and concerns.

I would meet or, more often, have a call with the chair of the audit committee before every meeting. We would agree on the agenda (I would always have a draft for him or her to review, change as necessary, and then approve), allocate time to each agenda item, and generally plan the meeting.

I never, *ever*, wanted to surprise the chair or any other member of the audit committee! I briefed the chair and relied on him or her to brief the other members. (That was always their preference.)

In addition to these calls, I would also have a longer call or meeting with the chair several times a year. Usually, they were at the corporate office

---

[95] By control environment, I refer to the COSO internal control component. I might, for example, share any concerns with management's commitment to internal control, the culture of the organization, and so on.

but on several occasions I would travel to meet him or her at their home or other convenient location.

The topics we covered in these periodic meetings varied depending on the state of the business, the concerns of the chair, and any matters I wanted to discuss.

But, we always spent time on the relationship. I needed to know how he felt about me and my team. Were we delivering the valuable information he or she needed to be effective in his or her oversight of the organization and its management? Were there areas where we could do more? Were we doing work that didn't matter?

Similarly, the chair needed to have confidence in me and my team. He or she needed to know that I was being totally open and holding nothing back. If I had concerns about executive management in general or with specific executives, he or she wanted and needed to know.

I also met one-on-one with the other directors. Again, those meetings were generally at the corporate offices but, from time to time, I would travel to a location convenient to them.

These meetings are, in my opinion and experience, essential.

They can also be highly enlightening!

I remember a one-on-one meeting in my office with one of the directors. We were having a convivial and open discussion, so I decided to ask a delicate question.

I told him that there is a saying "noses in, fingers out" when it comes to members of the board. It means that directors should ask penetrating questions to help them assess the competence of executive management, but they should never insert themselves to the point where they are making decisions that should be made by the management team. In other words, they should focus on gaining confidence in management and how they are handling situations and then leave them to do so.

After telling the gentleman about the saying, which made him laugh and then express his agreement with it, I said that I was used to audit committee members only asking the CFO high-level questions when he or she shared the financial results, forecasts, and so on. But, I had noticed that he and at least one other director asked many more detailed questions.

I asked whether this was because they were not satisfied with the answers, or whether they had some level of concern about the CFO himself.

The director just looked at me and smiled.

Words were not necessary.

Because every member of the audit committee received a copy of every audit report, and either I or the chair would talk to them before each meeting, I didn't need to consume a lot of their time at the regular audit committee meeting.

I am very much a believer that my job, in the main, is to help the audit committee discharge its oversight responsibilities effectively. That means that:

- I need to provide them with the information they need, when they need it, in a useful form
- I help them run efficient and effective meetings

This last point is one that I fear many overlook.

Audit committees have a huge set of responsibilities, but they only meet a few times each year and their meetings only last a few hours. While the number and length of meetings is increasing, according to studies, they don't really provide the directors with as much time as it perhaps should take for them to cover all the matters they should in sufficient detail.

As CAE, I was effectively the secretary of the audit committee meetings. Most of the time, I not only helped set the agenda and kept the minutes (subject to approval by the chair and the general counsel), but kept the meeting going. The chair would often rely on me to help him or her lead the meeting, keep everybody on point and on time, and ensure everybody who wanted to was able to contribute.

I have to say I enjoyed that task and the confidence in me the chair and other members demonstrated by letting me lead.

But, perhaps my greatest contribution was in keeping my own remarks short and concise.

As I said earlier, I usually didn't have a lot to share at the audit committee meeting that the directors didn't already know.

- They already knew about any significant risk or control issues. The meeting was an opportunity for them to ask questions and hear from management about those issues, not so much hear me repeat them.

- They had seen every audit report, so they didn't need to hear me tell them what they said. They didn't even need to see a summary.

- The directors knew I took a risk-based approach with a dynamic audit plan. I shared any major changes to the plan and gave them an opportunity to challenge me – which they rarely did. The members would ask management whether they agreed and, upon hearing that they did, would move on.

- Once a year, I would share my budget and plans. That would often merit a few minutes discussion, especially when management wanted to cut costs.

- Also once a year, I would share my overall assessment of the condition of internal controls and risk management – more on that momentarily.

As a result, my portion of the audit committee agenda (even when I had to report on the SOX program) was generally 15 minutes or less[96].

Taking more than 15 minutes wasted their time, because at that point I was not telling them anything they didn't already know – or needed to know.

Every minute I saved was a minute that could be spent on other matters, almost always more important than discussing an internal audit issue.

---

[96] On a few occasions, we spent far more time on audit issues. But that was only because those issues were important to the organization and the members of the audit committee.

In the same way that I saved their time and helped the directors be efficient by keeping my presentations short, I also kept the material I sent them for each meeting short.

I would normally help the general counsel collect and send to each director the pre-meeting materials.

I insisted that the materials had to be sent to the audit committee at least ten days prior to the meeting. We cannot expect them to have read the materials if they are not provided in good time.

It is a total waste of time for the directors to have the materials read to them at the board or committee meeting.

Board and committee time should be spent *discussing* the materials, not reading them.

It is essential not only that they be sent in good time, but they should not be excessive in length.

In my experience, it is not uncommon for a director to receive a book with several hundred pages of materials that they are expected to read, understand, and be ready to discuss at the meeting.

Most of the directors I worked with were not up to that inhuman task — and I can't say I am surprised.

It was a rare director[97] who could read and absorb several hundred pages. While most (I can think of one who gave up and came to the meeting unprepared) read the material, we still needed to review at least the highlights before we could have a productive discussion that would lead to an agreement on necessary actions.

---

[97] Jean-Francois Heinz, chair of the Business Objects audit committee, deserves special mention. Not only did he read everything he was sent, but when he arrived for the meeting his binder was marked-up and annotated with comments and questions. Often, he would call the CFO or me ahead of the meeting to get additional details or tell us he wanted to discuss something specific at the meeting.

Therefore, I took care to keep not only my oral presentation short, but the materials I included in the board briefing book were also short.

They were limited to what they needed to know, risks they needed to be aware of, management actions meriting their follow-up, and decisions requiring their input or approval.

On a few occasions, I would share reading or briefing materials with the committee. I would include them in the meeting materials if I felt that a short discussion around them would be beneficial. For example, I shared the COSO *Enterprise Risk Management – Integrated Framework* with the Business Objects audit committee with the suggestion that they review and discuss the Executive Summary.

However, my section of the audit committee was typically short.

I would usually have a 15-20 minute slot on the agenda, but would normally only speak for about 5 minutes, just to tell the members that we were on track and had no significant issues beyond what had been separately communicated. That would allow the directors to ask questions; if not, we could move on.

My annual report was longer. But I would speak for no more than 15-20 minutes unless there were extended discussions around the risk assessment, budget, or a change in my role (for example, should I assume new responsibilities[98]).

My 2000 year-end report was fairly typical. Its contents included:

- A high-level review of the work completed in 2000 (one page)

- Two pages on audit staffing (turnover rate, experience level, certifications, and diversity)

- A page each on internal audit and contracts audit (separate teams) and a paragraph on the investigations unit. These sections dived a little deeper into 2000 results

---

[98] Examples include starting a risk management function, an investigations unit, a contracts audit team, and assuming responsibility for the IT Quality Assurance function.

- Two pages on budget and related metrics (budget vs. actual; internal audit costs as a percentage of corporate revenue for the year by division and over time for the department as a whole; and, employees per internal auditor)

- A two-page discussion of changes planned for 2001

The report was a total of 9 pages.

My annual report also included a formal report on the overall condition of internal controls and the management of the more significant risks.

The annual report to the audit committee and top management was, in my opinion, the most important presentation I made each year.

Even though I had provided each of them with a copy of every audit report, and we had discussed any issues of significance as they arose, it was only during the annual report that I was able to tie all the audit work together.

This is the time when I would provide my key stakeholders with the *big picture* assessment of the management of risk and the effectiveness of internal controls they needed for their oversight of the organization.

I can remember the first time I made such a report to the Tosco Audit Committee.

They had seen, and we had discussed individually, a number of audit reports that were critical of operations at our Avon Refinery. However, when they heard me say that controls over major categories of objectives (such as compliance, efficiency of operations, and so on) were less than adequate they started asking critical questions of management.

The discussion between the board and management was not about individual controls or even individual audits. It was a strategic discussion.

The directors first asked management whether they agreed with my assessment of the operations at Avon, which they did. Management then explained why they were dissatisfied (which went further than what I had reported) and the steps they were taking to deal with the problem.

I believe that when internal audit enables such a strategic discussion, by sharing its assurance, insights, and advice, it is delivering the value that its stakeholders need.

It is world-class auditing, in my opinion. Certainly, that is how both management and the audit committee referred to the quality of our work: world-class.

## Maturity models

Sometimes, the best way to assess the adequacy of controls or the management of risk is through the use of a maturity model.

Perhaps the best use of this technique is when the area is relatively immature.

For example, if management has only recently started a risk management or information security function, it is unrealistic – and even unfair – to assess its current state as either 'adequate' or 'inadequate'. There should be no expectation that an embryonic function is already capable of meeting high quality standards.

An assessment that a new function has 'inadequate controls' does not give credit to its leaders for any progress they have made. In fact, it is downright discouraging. As I said, it is unfair to them.

It provides little value.

When I was a Vice President in IT with Home Savings of America, one of the functions that reported to me was the Information Security team. This was an area that I had built from nothing into a team of three experts who had implemented the ACF2 security system and several other measures. But, when we were audited after just one year of operation, the audit report gave us no credit for the work we had done; instead, it pointed out the areas we had yet to complete and concluded that security was inadequate.

The issues that the audit report raised were not only known to us, but were on the work plan that we provided to the internal audit team! All the recommendations in the audit report were already planned and had been included in our reports to senior management.

This report was of no value. It just made us angry.

What would have been useful would have been a report that informed management and the audit committee whether we were:

- Making the desired progress
- Adequately staffed and resourced
- Sufficiently supported by senior management
- Addressing the issues with an appropriate risk priority
- Completing each task with an appropriate level of quality

In other words, internal audit could have pointed out where we were on the path to effective information security that met the needs of the organization.

Such an audit report would have provided value to top management and the audit committee.

This is where a maturity model can be effective. IIA guidance has occasionally recommended the use of such a model, specifically for assessing risk management and certain governance processes.

I shared my maturity model for risk management in *World-Class Risk Management*. Here it is again, as an example.

| Maturity Level | Description | Key Attributes |
|---|---|---|
| One | Ad hoc | The management of risk is undocumented; in a state of dynamic change; and, depends on individual heroics. |
| Two | Preliminary | Risk is defined in different ways and managed in silos. Process discipline is unlikely to be rigorous. |

| Maturity Level | Description | Key Attributes |
|---|---|---|
| Three | Defined | A common risk assessment/response framework is in place. An organization-wide view of risk is provided to executive leadership. Action plans are implemented in response to high priority risks. |
| Four | Integrated | Risk management activities are coordinated across business areas. Common risk management tools and processes are used where appropriate, with enterprise-wide risk monitoring, measurement and reporting. Alternative responses are analyzed with scenario planning. Process metrics in place. |
| Five | Optimized | Risk discussion is embedded in strategic planning, capital allocation and other processes, and in daily decision-making. Early warning system to notify board and management to risks above established thresholds. |

An audit of risk management might report that maturity level three had been attained, the goal was to reach level four within the next year, and appropriate plans were in place to achieve that goal.

## Commentary

It is one thing to reach an assessment and develop our advice and insight. It is quite another to communicate that promptly, efficiently, and effectively to our stakeholders.

We are only effective when we not only perform quality work but provide the audit committee, executives, and operating management the information they need to be successful – when they need it, in a readily consumable and actionable way.

Every CAE should constantly re-evaluate the effectiveness of the department's communications.

The world is changing, and so must we. We must be ready and willing to set aside methods of the past and embrace the opportunities presented by the future, as we help our stakeholders lead the organization to success.

## Chapter 13: Fraud and compliance audits

A book about internal auditing that matters must address the role we can and should play when it comes to fraud. I will leave to others any detailed discussion of how to perform a fraud risk assessment or investigate potential theft and fraud. Instead, I want to discuss how the consideration of fraud should factor into internal audit design and planning.

I think there are several important points to consider when designing an internal audit function that strives for if not achieves world-class performance.

1. Internal audit is neither responsible for the design nor the operation of controls to prevent and/or detect fraud, waste, abuse, theft, and other breaches of the law or the organization's code of ethics[99].

2. The management of fraud risk, including the assessment of that risk, is a management responsibility.

3. The investigation of potential fraud is a management responsibility. However, certain types of potential fraud may be investigated by internal audit with the pre-approval of the audit committee.

4. Internal audit should consider fraud risk as part of its risk-based audit planning.

5. Internal audit should be careful about assigning more resources to fraud-related engagements than are justified by the level of risk to the organization's objectives.

6. The CAE should be careful not to allow fraud-related activities to create an environment of mistrust by management.

---

[99] I will refer to all of these as 'fraud' for convenience.

## When internal audit assumes fraud-related responsibilities

There is no single, right way to assign responsibilities between management and internal audit when it comes to fraud, except that internal audit should **never** be responsible for the design or operation of the controls that are relied on to prevent and/or detect fraud.

Internal audit may be relied upon by management to help them assess fraud risk. This is the case in many organizations, where the only fraud risk assessment is the one performed by internal audit.

I don't know whether management and the audit committee understand that they are relying on internal audit to perform what should, in theory, be a management activity. But, they are.

I consider this a 'consulting activity', permissible with the pre-approval of the audit committee.

Internal audit may also be relied upon to perform investigations of certain types of fraud. Again, I consider that to be a consulting activity and I have always included it in the internal audit charter, approved by the audit committee.

Some companies do not rely on internal audit for any fraud investigations. They have dedicated departments who conduct all investigations – and I am perfectly fine with that, with some provisos.

If another department performs fraud investigations, I believe internal audit should consider the risk to the organization if those investigations are not done well. They can lead to litigation by the individuals accused of misdoing, and that litigation and the business disruption it causes can be more costly than any loss from theft or fraud.

It may be necessary and appropriate, after assessing the fraud investigation risk, for internal audit to perform an audit of the fraud investigation unit. I would assess the:

- competence, experience, training, and certifications[100] of the individuals who perform or direct investigations;
- the independence and objectivity of the individuals and leaders of the department;
- the procedures followed in investigations, interviews and interrogations, and reporting to management;
- the process for determining whether there had be a breach of law or the code of conduct; and
- the process for determining the action to be taken once the investigation has concluded.

Internal audit is often the best source of expertise in investigating frauds such as conflict of interest; collusion with vendors, customers, or channel partners; travel and entertainment expense-related fraud; accounting and financial reporting fraud; and so on.

As CAE, I always worked closely with the general counsel and the head of Human Resources to define who would perform what types of fraud.

I do not believe internal audit should investigate charges of harassment, discrimination, or other human resources type of issues. Human Resources should have the ability to perform those investigations – I may need to audit that capability if the risk of a poor investigation is high.

If there is a security function that takes care of the physical security of the organization's facilities, they may be the best team to investigate theft. My audit team has assisted with those investigations from time to time, when we and the security function believed a joint effort is best.

We formalized the roles of each department in writing. This helps should there be any doubt over who does what[101], and we also inform

---

[100] I am an advocate of the Certified Fraud Examiner certification from the Association of Certified Fraud Examiners.

[101] At Business Objects, a new Senior Vice President of Human Resources initiated an investigation of a suspected financial irregularity, duplicating an existing audit investigation. When I found out, the HR investigation was shut down, although not before the SVP and I had a lively discussion.

employees whom they can contact if they wish to report potential violations of different sections of the code of conduct.

Over the years, I performed many investigations around the world and my team was responsible for many more. I shared stories about several of these in *World-Class Internal Audit: Tales from my Journey*. In that book, I described a set of principles, summarized as:

1.  Investigations should only be performed by individuals who have been sufficiently trained and experienced. When I formed a team at Tosco, one of the requirements was that the investigators hold a Certified Fraud Examiner (CFE) credential and had demonstrated, to my satisfaction, their abilities by performing investigations under the direct supervision of a CFE.

2.  It is critical to keep investigations confidential. There is a great risk to morale, let alone people's reputation and careers, when investigations are made public.

3.  The determination of whether a fraud has been committed is a legal responsibility. The investigator reports the facts, an attorney determines whether there has been a violation of the code of conduct and/or law, and management determines any disciplinary action.

4.  Although evidence will often build during an investigation that points to the 'guilt' of an individual or group, investigators should not allow themselves to start to believe in that guilt until all the evidence is in.

    Very often, the 'suspect' is not interviewed until late in the investigation so there is always a possibility that when he is interviewed additional evidence that points to innocence will be found. For example, I have seen and performed investigations where an individual did something that violated the code, only to find when he was interviewed that he did it at the express direction of his manager.

Fraud risk and the audit plan

The *Standards* have a number of references to fraud, including:

- **1210.A2** – Internal auditors must have sufficient knowledge to evaluate the risk of fraud and the manner in which it is managed by the organization, but are not expected to have the expertise of a person whose primary responsibility is detecting and investigating fraud

- **2120.A2** – The internal audit activity must evaluate the potential for the occurrence of fraud and how the organization manages fraud risk

- **2210.A2** – Internal auditors must consider the probability of significant errors, fraud, noncompliance, and other exposures when developing the engagement objectives

Where internal audit has confidence in the fraud risk assessment completed by management, I see no reason for audit to duplicate that assessment.

However, management may assume that the controls relied upon to manage fraud risk are operating effectively as desired.

Earlier, I talked about the Brisbane City Council approach where they consider the possibility that these controls are not functioning; they adjust the residual risk level bearing control risk in mind.

The CAE should consider fraud risk in developing the audit plan and the engagements it includes. But just because there is a fraud risk doesn't mean internal audit has to perform an audit of that risk.

Each risk should be prioritized based on its potential to affect the achievement of corporate objectives.

If fraud risk, or in practice a specific fraud scheme, rates high enough compared to other risks to the organization, engagements to address it should be on the audit plan.

If the risk is less than other organizational risks, I see no reason – other than top management or board request – to include it in the plan.

### Auditing compliance

I think of compliance in two ways:

- Compliance with company policy
- Compliance with applicable laws and regulations

I am not a fan of auditing compliance with company policy. It assumes that the policy is up-to-date and reflects what people should be doing.

My preference is to include an assessment in our audit of whether the company policy is appropriate and up-to-date rather than assuming it is. Only then do we assess compliance with policy.

As mentioned earlier, we live in a dynamic world and policies and procedures can be overtaken by events.

In *World-Class Internal Auditing: Tales from my Journey*, I shared this story of Laura Nathlich's audit of the Tosco Treasury function.

> The Treasurer at Tosco was a senior member of the Finance team, highly respected by company leadership. He had been a key member of the management team during the lean years at Tosco; shortly before I joined when the company was "leaking cash", he had led twice-daily meetings of the financial team to ensure there was sufficient cash to make it to the next day!
>
> So it was important that we make a good impression when we performed our first audit of his area.
>
> At the same time, he was a gruff curmudgeon (he reminded me of the late, great Alastair Sim as Scrooge in "A Christmas Carol") that scowled every time I saw him – and other executives told me that he shared that disposition with everybody except the CFO.
>
> So, I set the auditor, Laura Morton (now Nathlich), two tasks: the first was to perform an audit and provide an objective assessment of whether the Treasury function was meeting the needs of the corporation; the second was to get the Treasurer (Craig Deasy) to smile!

Laura exceeded my expectations (something she went on to do regularly).

As I had expected, Craig's area was in very good shape. It reflected his personality as a disciplined, careful individual that had a deep understanding of the business and its needs.

But, Laura identified one issue that only deepened Craig's frown.

She pointed out that the company's investment policy limited overnight investment of cash to the safest of all investments, which had the lowest of all rates of return. While this was the policy that had been approved by the board, the level of risk being taken (clearly a very conservative one) was inconsistent with the general attitude of the company to taking risk!

The company was a significant "player" in the commodity derivatives market, not only to hedge the price it would pay for its raw materials (crude oil) and the price it would obtain for its refined products (gasoline, diesel, jet fuel, and so on), but it also had a truly speculative position. (The manager in charge of our derivatives trading desk was permitted to make speculative trades of several million dollars, subject to supervision by Pete Sutton, a Vice President. Over the years, he was consistently profitable.)

So it was taking millions of dollars of risk in the commodities market but unwilling to take any risk in its overnight investments?

Laura recommended that the investment policy be reconsidered. That was a wise move. Only management can decide how much risk it is willing to take, but we (as the independent and objective internal audit team) can challenge them when appropriate.

Craig reluctantly agreed that Laura had a point – not on technical controls philosophy but on business grounds. He discussed it with the CFO and they agreed to change the policy.

I met with Craig and Laura to review the final report before it went to the audit committee. He gave Laura a reluctant smile and acknowledged that it was a professional audit.

The overnight investment policy was being complied with, but it was no longer appropriate to the business.

Internal auditors need to be free to approach every audit as business people, questioning every practice – is it right for the business?

The second form of compliance auditing focuses on the risk of non-compliance with applicable laws and regulations.

Where the risk justifies an audit (just like any other audit engagement, only risks that matter should be the subject of an audit) I will have my team focus on the controls that provide reasonable assurance that:

   a.   non-compliance will be prevented, and

   b.   any non-compliance will be detected promptly.

An audit that includes an assessment of whether the organization is actually in compliance is fraught with danger. If non-compliance is detected, what will the organization do? Will it have to report that to the regulators and will the report expose the company to action by the regulators? Can internal audit test all the activity and reach a conclusion that there has been no non-compliance?

I prefer to assess the controls and whether they provide *reasonable* assurance that non-compliance risk is managed effectively.

No company will have a stated risk appetite or tolerance when it comes to non-compliance. But the only way to ensure 100% compliance with all laws and regulations is, with very few exceptions, to close the company down. It's simply not doable.

You can come very close by having every activity double-checked and the checkers checked (to make sure they are checking properly). Maybe you need to have the checkers of the checkers checked. But at some point, the cost becomes absurd relative to the risk.

When assessing the management of compliance risk, I tend to ask what a reasonable, prudent official would find acceptable.

Commentary

Fraud is a very important topic for every internal audit department. As the *Standards* dictate, the risk of fraud must be a consideration in audit planning.

But, the level of resources dedicated to engagements around fraud should be consistent with the level of risk. Every hour on a fraud engagement is an hour that is not spent on another risk that matters, probably more than fraud.

After all, according to the 2016 report[102] issued by the Association of Certified Fraud Examiners, the median loss incurred is only $150, 000 with 23.2% of losses exceeding $1 million. While not insignificant, it is highly unlikely that a single fraud would merit the personal attention of the CEO or board.

I believe that every case of suspected fraud should be investigated, but I will only look at controls that provide fraud prevention and detection where the risk is high – and by that I mean that the risk is higher than other areas of risk.

Some audit departments have put analytics in place to detect fraud. I consider that a management responsibility. While the concept is attractive, and internal audit can make headlines by detecting fraud, we need to make sure at all times that we are auditing what matters most to the organization.

With respect to compliance audits, my preference is to audit the management of the risk of non-compliance. I think this is within internal audit's capabilities (although they may need to bring expert resources onto the team).

However, like any area of risk, I only perform compliance audits when they are either mandated by regulation or justified based on the level of risk.

---

[102] *Report to the Nations on Occupational Fraud and Abuse*

## Chapter 14: Independence and objectivity

Every internal audit department needs to be independent in fact and objective in appearance. Its effectiveness can be severely impaired if it is perceived as lacking in either, especially if that results in biased and/or unfair assessments.

The most critical test is whether internal audit is free from inappropriate influence by management (my phrasing). The IIA has published useful guidance[103] on the topic that explains the primary threats to independence and objectivity.

Some go too far.

They seem to treat independence as if it is something sacred.

I have even heard of an organization that refused to use any of the organization's existing reports because of 'independence issues'. So, they purchased an independent software package, wrote their own independent reports, and wasted corporate resources in the process. It's fine to test the integrity of reports before you use them, but this was way overboard.

No internal audit department can be pure when it comes to independence.

- We are employees of the company and receive compensation from the company.

- If the company fails, we lose our jobs.

- We report to the audit committee of the board, whose members are also compensated by the company.

- For those who seek advancement with the company beyond internal audit, there is always (even if subconscious) the knowledge that upsetting management could impair our future.

---

[103] A 2011 Practice Guide, *Independence and Objectivity*

- We have all heard of CAEs who have been dismissed, allegedly after running afoul of management.

We need to acknowledge this and deal with it.

If we feel unable to be independent and objective, we should seek another position.

At the same time, we should not shirk our responsibility to help the organization succeed.

Effective CAEs and staff will inevitably impress senior and executive management.

They should expect to be offered positions outside internal audit. They should also expect to be offered the opportunity to add responsibilities to their portfolio.

If a set of responsibilities can be added that neither detract from independence or objectivity, nor adversely affect the CAE's ability to lead the internal audit function, then the CAE should give them serious consideration.

In my career, I have taken on:

- A Contracts Audit function, where a separate team (later partially integrated with my internal audit leadership structure) audited compliance with our contracts by vendors. They also performed pre-audits of vendors and provided information to the procurement function that was used in contract negotiations and structure

- A Software License Compliance function; this team audited our customers and ensured they complied with the terms of the licenses for the software they purchased from us. The team worked closely with the sales and legal teams

- Leadership of the Risk Management function

- Chair of the Ethics Committee

- Responsibility for the IT Quality Assurance team

- Project management for the SOX program

### Commentary

What is a CAE to do if they cannot be independent of management?

I faced this problem at Solectron, where a new CFO (hired just months after me) changed my reporting from direct to the audit committee to direct to him, with no line to the board.

I admit that while I immediately started looking for a new position, I did not resign. Like most, I needed to support a young family.

Instead, I tried to build a relationship with the CFO and also with the audit committee members.

When challenged by the CFO, I stood my ground.

For example, at one time we were in the midst of investigating a number of small (thankfully not material) financial statement frauds. The CFO made it abundantly clear that he wanted me to stop, or at least pause the investigations while he negotiated a financing agreement. I decided that my obligation to the company and the board was to continue because at that point it was unclear how many of these small frauds we would uncover.

Almost everything worked out: we completed the investigations and the financing was achieved as desired. I say 'almost' because my relationship with the CFO was doomed and within a year I resigned.

Each CAE needs, in my opinion, to work with the board and executive management and remedy any serious impediment to his or her independence and objectivity.

Beyond that, each CAE must examine their conscience and act accordingly.

## Chapter 15: Embracing change

There's a saying: "think outside the box".

Certainly, when building or modifying an internal audit function, each CAE needs to "think outside the box". He or she needs to be able to discard, or at least set aside, traditional thinking – even their prior successful achievements.

The key is to design and then run an internal audit department that meets the current needs of the organization – and then be ready to change it as the needs of the organization change.

The trouble with people who think out of the box is that when they design a successful operation they often fall in love with it. They build a new 'box' and are unable to think outside it when times change.

Just because what you have worked well until now doesn't mean it is right for today and tomorrow.

We have to constantly challenge our success.

Is it still the best? How can we deliver more value to our stakeholders?

### A non-traditional delivery of assurance, advice, and insight

I have enjoyed talking over the years with Chris Keller, long-time CAE at Apple. Chris has definitely not only thought 'out of the box', but has stepped right out and kicked the box down. Over time, he has remade the Apple internal audit department into something I doubt can be seen anywhere else.

I first met Chris at a PwC-organized CAE roundtable in Silicon Valley. When I started questioning the value of traditional audit working papers, Chris said he rarely had working papers any more. In an environment such as at Apple, audits were not repeated and legacy working papers had next to no value. Most of his work was consulting in nature on Apple's major initiatives.

Chris and I chatted again about his department in 2015. His department is now 100% embedded into each of the major development teams. They advise management on risk and controls, monitoring to ensure that the project teams are not taking more risk than approved by the CEO and the board.

If one of his team believes the project is taking on more risk than top management would approve, the first step is a discussion with the senior executive in charge. If that doesn't resolve the issue, Chris is brought in.

Chris first talks to the senior executive. If that executive sticks to his guns, saying he is willing to take the risk, and Chris agrees with his auditor that the level of risk is higher than management desires, then Chris will 'invite' the executive to a meeting with the CEO. At this point, the executive will generally 'see the light'!

Chris has the total support and respect of the CEO and can initiate a meeting with very short notice, if any – because he is providing the valuable advice, assurance, and insight the CEO and the board need.

Although this may seem like a 100% consulting or advisory internal audit function, it is providing the assurance stakeholders need.

They know that Chris and his team are proactively involved, making sure that the more significant sources of risk are being managed at desired levels.

Adapt or be irrelevant

A July, 2016 Deloitte report[104] shared the results of a survey of over 1,200 CAEs. The theme was:

"Evolution or irrelevance"

Here are some quotes:

- Our research found that CAEs have serious concerns. They know that their organizations are changing—that's been the case for a while. They also know that Internal Audit needs to respond to meet the changing needs of their organizations.

---

[104] *2016 Global Chief Audit Executive Survey: Internal Audit at a crossroads*

Those organizations need Internal Audit to inform them about the future rather than only report on the past. They need insights as well as information, advice as well as assurance. They need reviews of not only financial and operational controls, but also of strategic planning and risk management processes. They need internal auditors to apply their rigor, objectivity, independence, and skills in new ways.

As the results of this survey indicate, Internal Audit will have to evolve in specific ways in order to meet these needs. The needed changes are clearer than ever. CAEs must now lead their functions to take the next critical steps. In addition, Internal Audit's key stakeholders, notably the audit committee and the executive team, must support the function as it takes those steps.

- The status quo is not an option when 85 percent of CAEs expect their organization to change moderately to significantly in the next three to five years, and nearly as many (79 percent) expect similar change in Internal Audit. The survey also found that most CAEs believe that management and the audit committee will expect Internal Audit to step up to meet new challenges

- Only 28 percent of CAEs believe that their functions have strong impact and influence within the organization. A disturbing 16 percent noted that Internal Audit has little to no impact and influence. Meanwhile, almost two-thirds believe that Internal Audit's strength in these areas will be important in the coming years. This disconnect—between current and needed impact and influence—must be addressed, for the good of Internal Audit and the organization.

- Dynamic reporting is poised to increase. Most Internal Audit groups communicate with stakeholders through static text documents and presentations. Use of text in particular is expected to decrease (from 78 percent to 58 percent) as dynamic visualization tools increase dramatically (from 7 percent to 35 percent). These dynamic visualization tools enable Internal Audit to deliver more insightful observations, interact with stakeholders, and deliver greater value.

- Reviews of strategic planning and risk management will increase. While about one third of Internal Audit groups have evaluated their organization's strategic planning process in the past three years, over half expect to do so in the next three to five years. A strong increase is also expected in the number of Internal Audit groups reviewing their risk management function.

- To make changes in its approaches and activities, Internal Audit should embrace an innovative mindset, as well as actual innovations. However, the function is not known for aggressive innovation.

- Perhaps Internal Audit should adopt the mantra of many companies—if you are not moving forward, you are moving backward, if only in relation to everyone who is moving forward.

This is all very consistent with my messages in this book and elsewhere.

## Commentary

We need to provide the assurance, advice, and insight our stakeholders need – and that means we have to audit what matters in a way and at a speed that delivers what they need when they need it.

When all around us is changing, especially when driven by technology, every CAE should be not only ready but eager to find a way to change.

We need to not only think out of the box every day, but every time we change we must be careful not to build a new box that will stifle innovation.

## Chapter 16: Closing thoughts

What does it all mean?

What is internal auditing that matters?

It's an internal audit function whose performance matters to key stakeholders on the board and in top management.

It's an internal audit function that provides the assurance that those key stakeholders need: assurance that they can rely on the organization's people, process, and systems to deliver on strategies and plans, achieve objectives, and deliver the desired level of value.

That assurance extends to the controls that ensure both the creation and preservation of value – controls that optimize performance and manage risks to objectives.

How is that achieved?

Internal audit must focus its time and resources on issues (i.e., risks and related controls) that matter to the board and top management.

It is not enough to say that internal audit is 'aligned' with the strategies and objectives of the organization. Internal audit's plans should be *driven* by those strategies and objectives, and the risks to their achievement.

It is not enough to assume that the best strategies and objectives have been established. Internal audit should always consider the possibility that defects in governance can lead to sub-optimal strategy-setting.

In fact, internal audit should always be thinking of the:

- Things that could go wrong and adversely impact the success of the organization – at a level that matters to the board and stakeholders, **and**
- what needs to go right if objectives are to be achieved.

Internal auditing that matters is focused on success (value creation) more than avoiding failure (value preservation). That is the only way an internal audit activity will gain the recognition it merits from the board and top management – because it helps them succeed.

Internal audit needs to adopt Lean thinking and eliminate all *muda* from its audit plan and processes.

Activities that do not contribute clear and meaningful value to the board and top management should be minimally questioned and optimally eliminated.

Internal audit needs to not only provide *assurance*, but all the advice and insight that can help the organization succeed.

While the *Standards* talk about "improving an organization's operations", a world-class internal audit activity, one that matters, enables more than incremental improvement. It helps the organization refine its operations to optimize the likelihood of success.

In order to deliver on this level of service, internal audit needs a world-class staff, managed at a similar level.

Nothing can beat the performance of high quality, motivated and empowered *thinking* people.

But that assurance, insight, and advice have no value unless the board and top management hear and listen to it.

Communications are vital.

The board and top management must receive the information they need when they need it, in a readily-consumed and actionable form.

All of this requires a departure from traditional methods. Fortunately, many organizations are on the path to excellence – a path that may have many stops along the way, but will continue as the need for change continues.

It is not clear what the future holds for business and organizations, let alone internal audit. Artificial intelligence, machine learning, and more promise improvements in decision-making, risk monitoring and management, and so on that could and likely will change our world yet again.

They key is to be vigilant and ready always to do what matters to the success of the organization.

## Acknowledgments

I have had the pleasure and privilege of working with and for many individuals over the years, each of whom influenced my thinking and practice of internal auditing.

This includes members of boards and audit committees; CEOs, CFOs and other top executives; CAEs for whom I worked; members of my various teams; and, CAEs and others with whom I networked through the IIA and elsewhere.

These are too many to mention here.

The individuals to whom I express a special 'thank you' are the expert practitioners who were kind enough to review a draft of this book. They caught not only editing mistakes, but other errors and omissions.

- John Fraser
- Steve Goepfert
- Larry Harrington
- Tom McLeod
- Patty Miller
- Michael Parkinson
- Dominique Vincenti

I also want to thank the Institute of Internal Auditors for granting permission for excerpts from the Standards and other materials to be included in this book.

## About the Author

**Norman Marks**, CPA, CRMA is a semi-retired chief audit executive and chief risk officer. He is a globally-recognized thought leader in the professions of risk management and internal auditing and remains an evangelist for "better run business", focusing on corporate governance, risk management, internal audit, enterprise performance, and the value of information. He is also a mentor to individuals and organizations around the world.

Norman has been honored as a Fellow of the Open Compliance and Ethics Group and an Honorary Fellow of the Institute of Risk Management for his contributions to risk management.

He is the author of four earlier books:

- *World-Class Internal Audit: Tales from my* Journey

- *Management's Guide to Sarbanes-Oxley Section 404: Maximize Value Within Your Organization* (described as "the best Sarbanes-Oxley 404 guide out there for management")

- *How Good is your GRC? Twelve Questions to Guide Executives, Boards, and Practitioners*, and

- *World-Class Risk Management*

Praise for *World-Class Internal Auditing: Tales from my Journey*, includes:

- "I thoroughly enjoyed Norman's book. My one regret is not buying it in hard copy, so I could tab it, highlight it, scribble in the margins, etc. It's the type of book I keep on my desk, available for quick reference or inspiration when the need arises. In his Introduction, Norman states his hope in writing World-Class Internal Audit is that it "...will amuse as well as provide some insights..." and that he wrote the book to "...stimulate some thinking..." I believe he succeeded on all three points.

  "World-Class Internal Audit is not a textbook or reference book containing audit programs or other details which can be used verbatim; there are many great resources available for this purpose. What I liked most about Norman's book is that the story of his personal career journey highly is relatable, despite being nothing like my own. He presents short stories about specific moments in his career with brutal introspection, explaining how he adapted or evolved his thinking along the way. His stories are relatable because they're not a load of hooey coming from on-high from an "all-knowing" internal-audit God; he is fallible, admits mistakes and missteps, and offers his lessons-learned. These stories lay the foundation for his view of World-Class Internal Audit and explain how he came to have this view."

- "Anyone that is passionate, motivated, and enthusiastic about the internal audit and enterprise risk management profession should read this book!

  "It will inspire you further to strive for continuous improvement, professional development, greater quality of the services you perform, and finally, it will infuse you with greater enthusiasm and determination in the pursuit of a world class internal audit organization."

Reviews for *World-Class Risk Management* include:

- Norman Marks' latest book "World-Class Risk Management" (2015) is a must read for anyone interested in this evolving topic. It will appeal to the beginner as it leads one from the basics through the various concepts and techniques, while it challenges the most serious practitioner to re-evaluate what they do and why. The academic will also benefit from using this book because of the exhaustive references to some of the best source material on this topic. Norman challenges many stereotypical and clichéd views on risk management, but keeps coming back to simple, easy to understand concepts. He captures the essence of his thinking in "The management of risk is an essential element in successful management." (page 13). This book makes you think, yet it is written in a lucid and friendly style. His thinking on 'risk appetite' challenges some 'sacred cows' held by many, but will help those who have struggled with this concept to find better ways of approaching this controversial subject. I wish he had written more on risk workshops but that may be another book someday. Well done, Norman, and thank you for sharing your experience, research and thinking.

- A very refreshing view of how risk management should be. Packed with a lot of good insights and force us to re-examine the way we think of risk management, its value to an organisation and to be relevant to the organisation objectives.

Norman's blogs are at normanmarks.wordpress.com and https://iaonline.theiia.org/blogs/marks.

63657416R00147

Made in the USA
Charleston, SC
07 November 2016